INTRODUCTION

No American president begins tenure in that office with a clean slate. Each enters the role equipped with a lens shaped by personal experience, expectations of a political party, and interpretations of what constitutes "the will of the people." Once in office, a president attempts to integrate these perspectives and develop an approach designed to transform current conditions into those the constituency considers more desirable. Even George Washington, as the first president, had to contend with the preexisting economic, military and political posture of a newly formed American state. The phenomenon of globalization further demands that each successive American president increasingly consider the international implications of domestic policy and the domestic implications of international policy. Thus, each president also inherits international conditions that must factor into their approach to governance. As President Obama entered his presidency, he did so in a context where the United States was already engaged in two wars within a backdrop of existing employment statistics, tax codes, health care structures, and national debt. The effects of the decisions made by President Obama when shaping these and other issues will, in turn, set the context within which his successor begins. Again, no president begins with a clean slate.

Harry S. Truman and Dwight D. Eisenhower were not immune to such complexities when they entered the Office of the President of the United States. Like all presidents before and since their tenures, they both brought personal and "party line" views to their presidencies as they began the process of shaping the national condition within preexisting domestic and international contexts. Truman would have to reframe his views of domestic policy in light of an international context of which he was largely unaware when he abruptly assumed office. Eisenhower would subsequently inherit the policies of Truman and reshape them in accordance with his views. Both presidents, however, began their first terms in office having to guide the military, the economy

1

and national security policy through the waning years of an unexpected war and into an era of dubious peace.

Truman and Eisenhower presided during an era that witnessed both a shift in the structure of global hegemony and the position of the United States within this new structure. Before the end of World War II, the Soviet Union had already begun to consolidate power and exert influence along its massive perimeter stretching from Eastern Europe to Northeast Asia. It soon became clear that the views and policies of Joseph Stalin would not be amenable to those of the United States and its Western Allies. In the wake of World War II, as Soviet power grew in the face of a British and French decline, the United States took the lead in representing and defending democratic values on the global stage. By 1947, a Cold War had begun and global power was now bipolar, shared between the United States and the Soviet Union. In this light, the reforming of national security policy took center stage in the Truman administration. As communist aggression became more dangerous with the acquisition of atomic power by the Soviets, and more brutally manifest with the onset of the Korean War, national security policy would remain paramount throughout Eisenhower's years as president.

This monograph explores the national security policies of Presidents Truman and Eisenhower. It focuses on how these policies affected the structures and budgets of the U.S. military, and its relationship with the national industrial base during the period of 1945 through 1960. Although the effect of policy on the U.S. Army is the specific focus of this monograph, general structural and budgetary changes within the other services are also presented. This monograph does not directly discuss the role of Congress in the shaping of national security during this period, nor does it discuss in detail elements outside of the conventional active duty military structure that may be relevant to national security, such as the National Guard, Reserves, or the Central Intelligence Agency. The focus is solely on the strategic policies implemented during this period from the view of the Truman and Eisenhower administrations, how these policies affected the active duty military structures and policies, and its relationship with the national industrial base.

This monograph comprises three main sections. The first section begins with the death of President Franklin D. Roosevelt and ends just prior to the onset of the Korean War. It explores how President Truman adopted and reshaped the policies of President Roosevelt regarding management of World War II and his plans for military demobilization and national reconversion following the war. This section then examines the effect of strategic policy on the posture of the military as the Truman administration perceived and responded to a growing communist threat.

The second section of this monograph begins with the onset of the Korean War and finishes with the end of the Truman administration in January 1953. It specifically explores the effect of strategic policy and federal military budgets on the training, equipment, and personnel postures of both the Republic of Korea (ROK) Army and the U.S. Eighth Army as the Korean War began. Also examined here is the response of the Truman administration to the North Korean invasion of South Korea, with a specific focus on how policies and budget supplementals enacted in the first year of the war stimulated the national industrial base to support military requirements throughout the remainder of the conflict.

The third and final section of this monograph examines how the Eisenhower administration reshaped the national security policies it inherited from the previous administration and the effects of these efforts on military structure, budget and interaction with the industrial base. Finally, this monograph concludes by comparing and contrasting how Truman and Eisenhower shaped inherited strategic contexts and policies and the effects of these policies on the military and its supporting industrial base. Also addressed is the relevancy of these conclusions in a modern context.

The key texts underpinning the research of this study comprise three broad categories: biographical studies and policy analysis of both Presidents Truman and Eisenhower; the interaction of strategic policy, military budgets and force structures during the Truman and Eisenhower administrations; the demobilization/mobilization processes and industrial base dynamics that occurred throughout the span of the Truman and Eisenhower administrations. Specific texts relevant to this study regarding the biographical and policy development analyses of President Truman include Alonzo L. Hamby's *Man of the People*, David McCullough's *Truman*, and Melvyn P. Leffler's *A Preponderance of Power: National Security, the Truman Administration, and the Cold War*. While McCullough's *Truman* presents fascinating insights into the persona of Harry Truman, and how his experiences shaped his views, Hamby's *Man of the People* offers a more detailed examination of Truman's policies, including his approach to reconversion.[1] Leffler's *A Preponderance of Power* provides a uniquely comprehensive exposition of events and processes leading to the strategic policy decisions of the Truman administration during the earliest years of the Cold War and the Korean War.

References key to this study regarding the biography and policy decisions of President Eisenhower include Jean Edward Smith's recently published biography of Dwight D. Eisenhower, *Eisenhower: In War and Peace*, Douglas Kinnard's *President Eisenhower and Strategy Management, A Study in Defense Politics*, and Robert R. Bowie and Richard H. Immerman's *Waging Peace*. Jean Edward Smith's recently published biography of Dwight D. Eisenhower, *Eisenhower: In War and Peace*, provides an in-depth view of Eisenhower's life and how his experiences shaped his views as President. *President Eisenhower and Strategy Management* by Douglas Kinnard is a succinct and clearly written study that explores the development and evolution of Eisenhower's New Look strategy and the coevolution of the military throughout his presidency. Robert R. Bowie and Richard H. Immerman's *Waging Peace* is an essential text for any study of Eisenhower's overall approach to national security strategy

---

[1]Alonzo L. Hamby, *Man of the People: A Life of Harry S. Truman* (New York: Oxford University Press, 1995). President Truman's approach to reconversion following World War II is presented in Chapter 21.

and the processes he implemented for its development. This text initially provides an overview of the policy of containment as it appeared during the Truman era, and then proceeds to present a detailed and fascinating account as to how Eisenhower integrated the concept into his Basic National Security Policy as it matured through the years of his presidency.

Numerous excellent references describing the interaction of strategic policy, military budgets and force structures during the Truman and Eisenhower administrations are available. References particularly helpful to this study regarding this topic include the first four volumes of the *History of the Office of the Secretary of Defense* series and the first volume of the *United States in the Korean War* series. The *History of the Office of the Secretary of Defense* series is intended to highlight civil-military relations, the effects of strategic policy on the military establishment, the role of the Office of the Secretary of Defense (OSD), and how the military and the OSD have evolved over time.[2] The first volume of this series, Steven L. Rearden's *The Formative Years, 1947-1950,* provides a thorough analysis of these issues during the Truman administration from the founding of the OSD in 1947 through the onset of the Korean War in June 1950. The second volume of this series, Doris M. Condit's *The Test of War, 1950-1953* explores the role of the OSD in shaping military strategy and budgets in response to the North Korean invasion of South Korea and their evolution throughout the remainder of the Truman administration.[3] Condit also discusses the role of the OSD in shaping the North Atlantic Treaty Organization (NATO) and the administration's response to the onset of the nuclear arms race that developed between the United States and the Soviet Union during this same period. The third and fourth volumes of this series, Richard M. Leighton's *Strategy, Money and the New Look, 1953-1956*, and Robert L. Watson's *Into the Missile Age, 1956-1960*, respectively, both provide

---

[2]Steven L. Rearden, *The Formative Years, 1947-1950* (Washington, DC: Historical Office, Office of the Secretary of Defense, 1984), ii.

[3]Doris M. Condit, *The Test of War, 1950-1953* (Washington, DC: Historical Office, Office of the Secretary of Defense, 1988), i.

detailed accounts of civil-military relations, military budget development, the conversion of strategic policy into military strategy, and how the OSD evolved during the New Look era of the Eisenhower administration.

Supplementing the detail provided to this study by the *History of the Office of the Secretary of Defense* series, which spans both the Truman and Eisenhower administrations, is James F. Schnabel's *Policy and Direction: The First Year*, the first volume of the *United States and the Korean War* series. This writing presents the evolution of U.S. strategic policy in the turbulent first twelve months of the Korean War and specifically focuses on how military leaders converted strategic policies into military strategy and operations from June 1950 through July 1951.[4]

The third category of texts underpinning the research of this study concerns the demobilization/mobilization processes and industrial base dynamics that occurred throughout the span of the Truman and Eisenhower administrations. Excellent references describing Truman's demobilization and reconversion policies include William G. Stewart II's *From War to Peace: A History of Past Conversions*, John Michael Kendall's doctoral thesis titled *An Inflexible Response* and Alonzo L. Hamby's *Man of the People*, described earlier in this introduction. Stewart's *From War to Peace* is a U.S. Government research study designed to compare four industrial and economic buildups and drawdowns in response to World War II, the Korean War, the Vietnam War and the Reagan administration.[5] Regarding its relevance to this monograph, this document serves as a useful tool to understand how the Truman administration adopted, shaped and executed the reconversion policies developed initially by the Roosevelt administration in the early years of World War II. Finally, Kendall's doctoral thesis, titled *An Inflexible Response,* first

---

[4]James F. Schnabel, *Policy and Direction: The First Year* (Washington, DC: Office of the Chief of Military History, United States Army, 1972), ix.

[5]William G. Stewart, *From War to Peace: A History of Past Conversions.* Annex B *to Adjusting to the Drawdown, Report of the Defense Conversion Commission* (Bethesda, MD: Logistics Management Institute, 1993), iii.

provides a general overview of the history of wartime manpower mobilization processes in the United States Army with a focus on the interwar period between World War II and the Korean War. Kendall further explores how the Army adjusted these processes in light of the unexpected onset of the Korean War and how these adjustments shaped manpower mobilization planning in the longer term.

Texts contributing significantly to this study regarding industrial base dynamics in response to strategic policies and war include James A. Huston's *Guns and Butter, Power and Rice: U.S. Army Logistics in the Korean War*, Elliot V. Converse III's *Rearming for the Cold War, 1945-1960* and Robert L. Watson's *Into the Missile Age, 1956-1960*, already described above. Huston's *Guns and Butter, Power and Rice* is an excellent reference that provides a thorough analysis of both the ROK and U.S. Army's sustainment postures as the Korean War began. Huston further provides outstanding insight as to how both the U.S. industrial base and the Army sustainment command structure responded to military war requirements and how their approaches evolved throughout the conflict. Converse's *Rearming for the Cold War, 1945-1960*, published in 2011, provides a chronological history and select case studies regarding the interactions between each of the Armed Services and the OSD as they pursued of the acquisition of major weapons systems during the Truman and Eisenhower administrations.[6] It is a comprehensive text that presents the technological evolution of the U.S. military within the backdrop of strategic policy, military budgets, acquisition processes, and interservice rivalries. *Rearming for the Cold War* is the first volume in the *History of Acquisition in the Department of Defense* series produced by the Historical Office of the OSD.

---

[6]Elliott V. Converse III, *Rearming for the Cold War, 1945-1960* (Washington, DC: Historical Office, Office of the Secretary of Defense, 2011), v.

APRIL 1945 – JUNE 1950

Truman's First Tasks: End the War, Demobilization and Reconversion (April 1945-Jan 1947)

With the passing of Franklin D. Roosevelt on 12 April 1945, Vice President Harry S. Truman became President of the United States. There were multiple pressing matters to address. Before addressing any of them, however, his first task was to learn of what the matters actually consisted. He had been Vice President for less than three month, inexperienced in foreign policy and uninformed by Roosevelt on the details of most international issues.[7]

Truman was aware of the most pressing international and domestic issue – winning the war. With an Allied victory all but assured in the European theater, staunch Japanese resistance became the focus of his war-related concerns. Less than four months into his Presidency, Truman hoped to prevent what some advisors predicted as many more months of intense fighting and perhaps a quarter of a million more U.S. dead in the Pacific theater.[8] He approved the use of atomic weapons against Japan. For Truman, the challenge of winning the war rapidly transitioned to the greater challenge of establishing an enduring peace.

Although international security issues would come to dominate much of the Truman's efforts in the coming years, his immediate focus was domestic in nature.[9] The short-term goals included the rapid demobilization of the military and the reconversion of industry from large-scale military-directed production back to a civilian market demand-based economy. This had to be accomplished while simultaneously preventing rampant inflation and unemployment.[10] The ensuing integration of over ten million veterans into the civilian work force in less than a year was unprecedented and potentially devastating. Many in Truman's administration believed that a

---

[7]Melvyn P. Leffler, *A Preponderance of Power: National Security, the Truman Administration, and the Cold War* (Stanford, CA: Stanford University Press, 1992), 26.

[8]David G. McCullough, *Truman* (New York: Simon & Schuster, 1992), 438-439.

[9]Hamby, *Man of the People*, 361.

[10]Ibid., 362-363.

lack of detailed fiscal planning during World War I facilitated latent economic conditions that eventually materialized and culminated in the Great Depression of the 1930's.[11] Truman was determined to prevent another such occurrence. Fortunately, the Roosevelt administration, still essentially in place, had begun postwar planning in November 1940, over a year *before* American entry into the war.[12]

The organizations leading the reconversion planning and execution efforts at the national level took many forms throughout World War II and their objectives were twofold. The first objective was enhancing the ability of veterans to reintegrate into the workforce while the second objective was facilitating the timely reconversion of government-contracted industries back to meeting the demands of a peacetime civilian economy.[13] To be successful, this second objective required a carefully phased contract termination process that eventually had to address over 300,000 contracts worth more than $65 billion (over $800 billion in current U.S. dollars).[14] The Roosevelt administration began this process ten months *before* the Normandy invasion and by November 1945 less than 20,000 contracts worth less than $1 billion remained.[15]

Despite these few examples of the Roosevelt administration's successful reconversion planning efforts, Truman would have little else with which to move forward at the conclusion of the war.[16] Thus, by 6 September 1946, Truman developed and delivered to Congress a 21-point program outlining his own extensive plans for reconversion.[17] Although Truman would find himself intervening in nationwide labor struggles, an international food crisis, and brief periods of

---

[11]Ibid., 361-362; Stewart, *From War to Peace*, 4-5.

[12]Stewart, *From War to Peace*, 5.

[13]Ibid., 6-8.

[14]Ibid., 8.

[15]Ibid., 9.

[16]Hamby, *Man of the People*, 375.

[17]Ibid., 362.

inflation over the next twelve months, his efforts averted massive unemployment, long-term

inflation and a post-World War II economic depression.[18]

Although the Roosevelt administration did initiate some of the economic reconversion

efforts that extended into the Truman presidency, military demobilization was a task for which

execution remained entirely under the purview of Truman. However, demobilization also had

planning efforts that preceded America's entry into the war. Unfortunately, these planning efforts

were more ostensible than real.

In February 1941, Army Chief of Staff General George C. Marshall recalled to active

duty Brigadier General John McAuley Palmer, one of the architects of National Defense Act of

1920, to serve as a special advisor on demobilization.[19] In July 1943, General Marshall took an

additional step in this direction and formed the Special Planning Division. Marshall specifically

tasked this austere group of twenty officers with formulating military demobilization plans.[20]

Although it created the Special Planning Division on its own accord, the War Department

marginalized its efforts during the war.[21] Further, the lack of a coherent national security strategy

forced this group to work in a vacuum.[22] Neither the State nor War Department provided the

Special Planning Division with a vision of future world conditions or budgetary considerations

for use as parameters within which to plan.[23] In fact, the only real guidance came from Marshall

himself that he based solely on an anticipated significant reduction in peacetime funding. The

---

[18]Ibid., 384-385.

[19]John Michael Kendall, "An Inflexible Response: United States Army Manpower Mobilization Policies 1945-1957" (Ph.D. Dissertation, Duke, 1982), 43; William W. Epley, *America's First Cold War Army, 1945-1950* (Arlington, VA: Institute of Land Warfare, Association of the United States Army, 1999), 2.

[20]Epley, *America's First Cold War Army*, 2.

[21]Kendall, "An Inflexible Response", 47.

[22]Epley, *America's First Cold War Army*, 3.

[23]Ibid.

eventual peacetime Army, Marshall concluded, needed to consist of 330,000 volunteer troops.[24]

The plan further assumed a one-year warning for crisis mobilization, where National Guard units

filled war requirements until the Universal Military Training (UMT) program provided the

backfill.[25] Congress, however, had not approved UMT and its $1.75 billion price tag.[26] Thus, the

Special Planning Division created a post-war vision of the Army that, although approved by

Marshall himself before he retired in November 1945, both the Truman Administration and the

Army largely ignored for being too vague and outmoded.[27]

Thus, unlike the economic and industrial sectors, the Army began demobilization almost

from scratch on 1 September 1945. It began with a personnel strength of over eight million

(including Army Air Forces), $50 billion in total equipment, eighty-nine divisions of organization

and no approved or executable plan.[28] Furthermore, the Fiscal Year (FY) 1946 Total Obligation

Authority (TOA) budget for the Army (and Army Air Forces) was $21.9 billion, down from

$51.9 billion for FY 1945.[29] Another view reveals that overall military spending as a percentage

of the Gross National Product (GNP) dropped from 36.7% in FY 1945 (GNP = $213.4 billion) to

20.7% in 1946 (GNP = $212.4 billion).[30] These initial conditions set the stage for a

demobilization process about which General Marshall later quipped, "It was no demobilization. It

was a rout."[31]

---

[24]Kendall, "An Inflexible Response", 54.

[25]Ibid., 56.

[26]Epley, *America's First Cold War Army*, 8.

[27]Ibid., 5.

[28]Kendall, "An Inflexible Response", 53.

[29]United States Department of Defense, *National Defense Budget Estimates for FY 2000* (Washington, DC: Department of Defense, 1999), 84.

[30]Rearden, *The Formative Years*, 310; Stewart, *From War to Peace*, 3.

[31]Ed Cray, *General of the Army: George C. Marshall, Soldier and Statesman* (New York, NY: Cooper Square Press, 2000), 628.

With demobilization formally initiated on 1 September 1945, the Army began

discharging soldiers at the rate of 1.2 million soldiers per month. This continued through January

1946 when new revisions, implemented by the new Chief of Staff of the Army, General Dwight

D. Eisenhower, curbed the process. Eisenhower was alarmed at the pace and believed that, if left

to continue, it would threaten his ability to fulfill occupation requirements in Germany and

Japan.[32] By this time, demobilization efforts reduced the Army to nearly half its strength of 8.3

million troops in June 1945 to 4.2 million.[33] Even with these new revisions in place, however, the

Army (and Army Air Forces) personnel strength dropped to 1.8 million in the next six months.[34]

As a less robust force of minimally trained new recruits replaced the skilled veterans that were

leaving the service in droves, the remaining Army equipment had little chance of receiving proper

maintenance.[35] Further, with the likelihood of relatively miniscule Army budgets in the coming

years, the procurement of new equipment was also remote. In fact, the combined TOA budgets

for Army (and Army Air Forces) for the procurement and research, development, test and

evaluation (RDT&E) programs in FY 1946 was $3.2 billion, down from $25.5 billion in FY

1945.[36]

Truman Moves Forward: The Growing Communist Threat (Jan 1947-June 1950)

President Truman was aware of ongoing Soviet pressure in the Balkan states and Eastern

Europe, as well as its ambitions in Asia, since his first briefings as President. In these same

briefings, Truman's advisors also made him aware that these vague Soviet objectives may not

---

[32]Epley, *America's First Cold War Army*, 4-5.

[33]Craig A. Harding, "Budgeting for the Nation's Defense Following the End of National Conflicts" (Master's Thesis, School of Advanced Air and Space Studies, 2009), 37.

[34]U.S. Department of Defense, *National Defense Budget Estimates for FY 2000*, 208.

[35]James A. Huston, *Guns and Butter, Powder and Rice: U.S. Army Logistics in the Korean War* (Selinsgrove: Susquehanna University Press, 1989), 25.

[36]U.S. Department of Defense, *National Defense Budget Estimates for FY 2000*, 144, 156.

only be attainable but in direct conflict with American interests and values.[37] The USSR, they

advised, would become the only economic and military rival to the United States after the war.[38]

Indeed, Stalin viewed the ensuing chaos of the final months of World War II in Europe and the

Pacific as an opportunity for a Soviet land-grab. Stalin's apparent initial goal was to establish a

security zone buffer and regions of influence along the entire stretch of the Soviet Union's

immense borders.

The cracks in any long-term American-Soviet unity began to form almost immediately.

In early May 1945, there were two ceremonies for the German surrender to the Allies: one in

Berlin with the Soviet Union, and one in France with the remainder of the Allies.[39] Within

months, significant friction developed between American and Soviet military units operating in

occupied Germany regarding the movement of the British and American units across the Soviet

zone into West Berlin.[40] Stalin applied pressure to both Greece and Turkey in the form of support

for communist insurgencies and demands for territorial concessions, respectively. During the

final days of the war in the Pacific in August 1945, a stubborn and brutal Soviet occupation of

northern Korea successfully reestablished a Korean Communist Party in Pyongyang.[41] From mid-

January through early February 1946, American and Soviet military leaders held fifteen sessions

in Seoul to discuss the future governance of the peninsula nation. The U.S. agenda included

facilitating a unified, independent Korea and a combined U.S.-Soviet plan to assist Korea in

development and reform. These sessions produced no agreements.[42] By the end of January 1946,

it became clear that Stalin was intentionally delaying the withdrawal his of his forces from Iran in

---

[37]Leffler, *A Preponderance of Power*, 35.

[38]McCullough, *Truman*, 372-373.

[39]John Lewis Gaddis, *The Cold War: A New History* (New York: Penguin Press, 2005), 6.

[40]Jonathan M. House, *A Military History of the Cold War, 1944-1962* (Norman, OK: University of Oklahoma Press, 2012), 113-114.

[41]Allan Reed Millett, *The War for Korea, 1945-1950: A House Burning* (Lawrence, KS: University Press of Kansas, 2005), 49-52.

[42]Ibid., 73.

spite of agreed upon timelines with Iran, the United States and Britain.[43] Prodding by the newly

established United Nations on this issue produced no immediate response from Stalin, only

withdrawal several months later.[44]

In February 1946, with demobilization continuing at a furious pace, George F. Kennan,

the U.S. Minister-Counselor in Moscow, cabled the renowned "Long Telegram" to his State

Department seniors in the Truman administration. It was an effort to warn of, explain, and

perhaps even forestall, what he already sensed as the onset of long-term hostile U.S.-Soviet

relations. Although some have interpreted the document as a subtle call to arms against the

Soviets, Kennan himself later noted that his intent with the telegram (and the subsequently

published "X article") was not to suggest a deliberate escalation towards war with the Soviet

Union, but rather "a plea" to use "political resistance" instead.[45] In any case, Kennan's prediction

of a worldwide U.S.-Soviet standoff simply helped to confirm what the Truman administration

was already beginning to understand.[46] In fact, a memorandum submitted to Truman in May 1945

by the director of the Office of Strategic Services (OSS), William J. Donovan, already provided a

similar detailed view of global Soviet ambition and captured the essence "containment" before

Kennan's cable.[47] This memorandum further suggested that since the Soviets would avoid war for

at least another ten years, the United States should capitalize on that interval by responding to

Soviet aggression with action that is "clear, firm, and thoroughly non-provocative" while

simultaneously providing active support to U.S. interests and allies across Europe and Asia.[48]

---

[43]Robert J. Donovan, *Conflict and Crisis: The Presidency of Harry S. Truman, 1945-1948* (Columbia, MO: University of Missouri Press, 1996), 158.

[44]Gaddis, *The Cold War*, 28.

[45]Rearden, *The Formative Years*, 8.

[46]Donovan, *Conflict and Crisis*, 187.

[47]Leffler, *A Preponderance of Power*, 60-61.

[48]Ibid., 61.

Continued demobilization efforts, significant reductions in military spending, and the economic nature of both the Truman Doctrine and Marshall Plan suggest that Truman heeded both Kennan and Donovan's suggestion of using political resistance and "non-provocative" action toward the Soviets instead of pure military power in the coming years. With the exception occupation duties in the European and Far East Commands and the establishment of military advisory groups in Greece and Turkey in 1947, the Truman administration did not ask much of the Army, or the military in general, in its approach to the deepening Cold War of 1947.

In late September 1947, in an effort to remain within budget, the newly formed Defense Department looked to see from where it could reassign troops to more pressing locations on the globe.[49] The 45,000 troops remaining in Korea since the end of World War II became an easy target. Despite warnings that a withdrawal of these troops would lead to a communist takeover of the peninsula from both the Central Intelligence Agency (CIA, formerly the OSS) and a military assessment completed by General Wedemeyer at the special request of President Truman, Army leadership decided their withdrawal would commence anyway in September 1948.[50]

Three events occurred in 1948 that began to change the Administration's view on defense spending and its diplomatic approach to confronting global communist expansion.[51] In February, a Soviet-backed communist seizure of power occurred in the sole remaining democracy of Eastern Europe, Czechoslovakia.[52] In early March, General Lucius Clay, the U.S. Military Governor in Germany forwarded what would become known as "war warning" to Washington. In his telegram, General Clay stated that, although he had no direct evidence of any specific upcoming Soviet military action, he sensed a "feeling of a new tenseness in every Soviet

---

[49]Rearden, *The Formative Years*, 257.

[50]Ibid., 261.

[51]Epley, *America's First Cold War Army*, 15.

[52]Gaddis, *The Cold War*, 32-33.

individual with whom we have official relations."[53] Less than four months later, in late June, a Soviet-enforced surface blockade of Berlin commenced.[54] With both events occurring in Europe, the withdrawal of 45,000 U.S. troops from Korea began as scheduled three months later in September 1948.[55]

During the withdrawal of U.S. troops, the Korean peninsula formally divided into two republics separated along the Thirty-eighth Parallel. In August 1948, the Korean leadership structure south of the parallel transitioned from a U.S. military government to the Republic of Korea (ROK), henceforth referred to here as South Korea. In September 1948, Koreans north of the 38th parallel established the "communist-dominated regime" of the Democratic People's Republic, henceforth referred to here as North Korea, which claimed "jurisdiction over all Korea."[56] By November 1948, only the 7,500 troops of the Fifth Regimental Combat Team (RCT) from the Seventh Infantry Division remained in South Korea.[57] The Army kept this force in place only as a response to rumors of an imminent North Korean invasion.[58]

In January 1949, General Lawton Collins, the Army Chief of Staff, reengaged General MacArthur, the Commander in Chief, Far East Command, on the need for retaining the Fifth RCT in South Korea. Although the CIA believed they should remain in place to help quell South Korean revolts and bolster South Korean forces as an effective deterrent to a communist takeover there, General MacArthur recommended otherwise. He believed that even with U.S. training and equipment, South Korean forces had little chance of defeating a full Soviet invasion, but were currently capable of handling all other contingencies below this level.[59] Furthermore, he argued,

---

[53]Rearden, *The Formative Years*, 281; Millett, *A House Burning*, 186.

[54]Rearden, *The Formative Years*, 288.

[55]Ibid., 261.

[56]Ibid.

[57]Millett, *A House Burning*, 186.

[58]Rearden, *The Formative Years*, 261.

[59]Millett, *A House Burning*, 186.

such a small number of remaining U.S. troops would do little to defeat such an attack and, therefore, should redeploy from the peninsula in May 1949. The Army completed its withdrawal on 29 June 1949, repositioning the Fifth Regimental Combat Team from South Korea to Hawaii.[60]

On 23 September 1949, Truman announced to the nation the successful development of a Soviet atomic bomb one month earlier.[61] A week later, on 1 October, Mao Tse-tung announced a communist victory in China and established the People's Republic of China. Months before, Mao declared that, unlike Tito in Yugoslavia, he intended to forge relations with Moscow and form "an international united front."[62] Stalin responded by announcing a "division of labor" approach between the Soviet Union and China whereby the USSR would focus its efforts on influencing Europe while China does the same in Asia.[63] In January 1950, with American support for South Korea appearing to decline rapidly, Stalin agreed to support Kim Il-sung, the North Korean president, in his efforts to unify the peninsula under communist rule.[64]

The Administration spent the spring of 1950 mostly debating its approach to a final Japanese peace treaty. Most of the concern regarded avoiding the provocation of a Soviet attack on Japan by not including them in the treaty process, subsequently removing U.S. troops and leaving Japan vulnerable.[65] The other significant effort within the Administration that spring was the drafting of yet another new approach to addressing communism. The National Security Council document known as NSC-68 captured that effort. In addition to recommending significant increases in funding to a multitude of indirect approaches for combating communism

---

[60]Rearden, *The Formative Years*, 264.

[61]Millett, *A House Burning*, 230.

[62]Gaddis, *The Cold War*, 37.

[63]Ibid., 39.

[64]Ibid., 41-42.

[65]Leffler, *A Preponderance of Power*, 347.

already in existence, it also obscurely proposed the idea of using conventional military force in "local situations", or put another way, by engaging in "limited wars."[66] North Korea, now confident with the promise of Soviet and Chinese support, would soon present an opportunity for the United States to implement this "limited war" concept with its invasion of South Korea on 25 June 1950.

Shaping the Army: January 1946-June 1950

The post-World War II demobilization began on 1 September 1945 and continued until 30 June 1947.[67] From 1 September 1945 through 1 January 1946, Army personnel strength dropped from 8.3 million troops to 4.2 million.[68] During this time, Army Chief of Staff General Eisenhower contemplated the shape of a peacetime military establishment. In February 1946, Eisenhower submitted to the Joint Chiefs of Staff (JCS) a general vision of a future global and total war that would last up to five years, similar to World War II, but one in which the United States may not have allies.[69] Over the next several months, the Army staff supplemented this scenario with planning and refinement that considered budgetary constraints and mobilization capabilities. The plan approved by Army headquarters in September 1946 proposed a Regular Army endstrength of 1.07 million troops by 1 July 1947 with a reserve process capable of expanding this force to "4.5 million (fifty-six divisions) within twelve months."[70] However, as demobilization wound down, and with over 400,000 troops transferred to the Air Force, Army strength stood at 684,000 spread across twelve divisions by July 1947.[71] Further, the FY 1948

---

[66]Ibid., 356, 360.

[67]Epley, *America's First Cold War Army*, 4.

[68]Harding, "Budgeting for the Nation's Defense", 37.

[69]Kendall, "An Inflexible Response", 57-58.

[70]Ibid., 58.

[71]Ibid., 89; Epley, *America's First Cold War Army*, 6.

TOA budget for the Army now stood at $3.2 billion, down from $5.9 billion the year before.[72] With falling budgets, failing recruitment and reenlistment efforts, the Army rolls dropped to 538,000 spread across ten divisions by June 1948, over 120,000 below plan.[73] The majority of these divisions were understrength, undertrained, with poorly maintained equipment procured during World War II.

In the summer of 1947, Congress and President Truman both initiated separate panels to determine the future role of air power and develop policies of both civilian and military aviation. Because of its obvious link to the strategic employment of atomic power through long-range bombers, these investigations concluded that national military defense planners should now use air power, both Air Force and naval, as the basis of their planning.[74] With perceived shortages in both aircraft and aviation organizations in the Air Force and Navy, Congress would direct military budgetary efforts to these areas. Additionally, in February 1948, General LeRoy Lutes, Staff Director of the Munitions Board, raised the concern that the Army would likely be unable to equip over half of its active and reserve combat divisions in the event of mobilization.[75] As communist aggression intensified in 1948 with Soviet actions in Czechoslovakia and General Clay's "war warning" from Germany, civilian and military leaders became more amenable to increased defense spending.[76] Congress responded the Army and Air Force materiel concerns by supplementing the FY 1948 military budget in April 1948, but with all additional funds appropriated to the Air Force.[77] The Army, however, would receive its increase in FY 1949 TOA budget to over $4 billion, nearly a $1 billion increase over its FY 1948 budget of $3.2 billion.[78]

---

[72]U.S. Department of Defense, *National Defense Budget Estimates for FY 2000*, 84.

[73]Epley, *America's First Cold War Army*, 4, 11.

[74]Rearden, *The Formative Years*, 316.

[75]Ibid., 317.

[76]Epley, *America's First Cold War Army*, 15.

[77]Ibid.

[78]U.S. Department of Defense, *National Defense Budget Estimates for FY 2000*, 208.

In June 1948, just before the onset of the Soviet blockade of Berlin, Truman and Congress addressed the manpower shortages by signing into law the Selective Service Act and invigorating a peacetime draft. Its effect was an increase in the Army rolls by 121,000 troops in the next twelve months to an overall strength of 659,000 by June 1949, but still 131,000 short of the FY 1949 goal of 790,000 as requested by Secretary of Defense James Forrestal and approved by Congress.[79] However, despite the acquisition of atomic power by the Soviets and a communist victory in China, both of which occurred in the fall of 1949, Congress was not convinced of an imminent communist threat and defense budgets for FY 1950 declined. Accordingly, Army strength declined from 659,000 in June 1949 to 591,000 by June 1950.[80]

Finally, throughout the years of 1946-1949, both Army procurement and research, development, testing and evaluation (RDT&E) programs were nearly non-existent. The combined procurement and RDT&E budget of $15.1 billion in FY 1945 dropped to $725 million in FY 1946, $201 million in FY 1947 and $157 million in FY 1948.[81] In FY 1949, the combined budgets for these areas increased to $428 million. The Army expended the procurement funds allocated to these budgets to mostly to aid requirements in support of Marshall Plan programs in occupied areas while RDT&E funds mostly supported guided missile research and atomic energy programs in an effort to remain competitive with the other services.[82] Meanwhile, the Army was still equipped mostly with the older M4 model Sherman tank while production of the newer M26 design that would prove so effective in the coming war had, in fact, stopped by 1947.[83]

By June 1950, the American military presence in Korea, once represented by the Sixth and Seventh Infantry Divisions under the United States Army Forces in Korea (USAFIK), now

[79]Epley, *America's First Cold War Army*, 16.

[80]Ibid., 18.

[81]U.S. Department of Defense, *National Defense Budget Estimates for FY 2000*, 144.

[82]Epley, *America's First Cold War Army*, 20.

[83]Ibid.

appeared as the Korean Military Advisory Group (KMAG). This organization, referred to as "Kiss My Ass Good-bye" by some, consisted of a little over five hundred officers and enlisted men. Brigadier General William L. Roberts, KMAG's first commander, stated that the organization primary purpose was for training Republic of Korea Army (ROKA) officers at the regimental level so they could, in turn, train their men.[84] Since July 1949, KMAG operated under a contingency plan not shared with its ROKA counterparts.[85] The crux of the plan, known as OPERATION CRULLER, stated that in the event of a crisis, KMAG, along with Ambassador John Muccio and his diplomatic mission, would evacuate the Korean peninsula and leave behind the South Korean troops its mission was to advise and assist.[86]

JUNE 1950 – JANUARY 1953

Strategic Visions Meet Reality – 25 June 1950

Truman's first five years as President presented him with a global strategic environment where political change and extensive threats to American ideals developed rapidly. In this relatively short period, Communism appeared to flourish across much of Europe and Asia as it tried to fill the voids where waning British and French colonial power once existed. The Middle East experienced increasing tensions as seemingly incompatible religions fought over holy territories laden with vast stores of subterranean oil. Concurrently, Soviet atomic technology continued to progress. The pace and complexity of these events likely hindered Truman in developing a clear strategic vision from which the military could derive conceptual guidance following World War II. Although Truman was clear in that he believed American power and influence derives as much from a strong domestic economy, balanced budgets and international

---

[84]Millett, *A House Burning*, 213-214.

[85]Ibid., 241.

[86]Ibid.

21

economic aid as it does military might, the only guidance for Army planners during these years was continuing occupational duties in Europe and Japan and constrained budgets.

Although the standing peacetime military strength in June 1950 was 1.4 million, in fact three times larger than the pre-war 1940 military, with the Army just under three times larger at 591,000 troops, military budgets over this same period did not increase proportionately.[87] With the combination of inflation and the rising costs of more advanced military hardware, mostly aviation related, the purchasing power of the military was "greatly diminished" despite seemingly larger budgets as compared to pre-war periods.[88] In absolute terms, many doubted whether this peacetime Army, while admittedly unprecedented in size, was still proportionate to both requirements of an expansive occupational mission and providing protection against unforeseen threats.

Even after Truman acknowledged a requirement for rearmament beginning in FY1949 due to Soviet aggression in Eastern Europe, he preferred a "slow, steady" approach stretching several years with an emphasis on air power to exploit the American atomic monopoly.[89] Such an approach, Truman believed, would help to prevent federal deficit spending while not signaling military mobilization to the Soviet Union.

To make his point, Truman firmly capped the defense budget for FY 1949 at a little over $13 billion and at $15 billion for FYs 1950 and beyond.[90] It is here that Truman truly began "perpetuating the gap between means and ends" by simultaneously approving the broad anticommunist objectives found in National Security Council policy paper 20/4, while limiting

---

[87]U.S. Department of Defense, *National Defense Budget Estimates for FY 2000*, 208; Rearden, *The Formative Years*, 310.

[88]Rearden, *The Formative Years*, 310.

[89]Leffler, *A Preponderance of Power*, 227; Rearden, *The Formative Years*, 316, 338.

[90]Rearden, *The Formative Years*, 327-328.

the military capabilities likely required for doing so.[91] General Thomas B. Larkin, assistant chief

of staff for logistics, highlighted this gap on 7 June 1950 when he stated, in reference to the

Army's overall materiel readiness, "Had war occurred this morning we would have to wage it for

a long period with our World War II equipment. Much of this is verging on obsolescence. Most

of it requires extensive repair and overhaul."[92]

Less than three weeks later, on 25 June 1950, the North Korean army would confirm the

accuracy of General Larkin's comments as it rushed across the Thirty-eighth Parallel into South

Korea. The warning and recommended approaches to the growing communist threat cloaked in

NSC 68 simply came too late for an effective and timely bridging of this gap. Although the policy

was complete nearly three months before the North Korean invasion, the Truman administration

had not yet approved or funded it by the outset of war.[93]

Four days after the invasion, on 29 June, as 2,000 American civilians, government

employees, and military personnel evacuated South Korea to Japan, MacArthur flew in the

opposite direction to assess the situation first hand. His assessment convinced Truman to

authorize the commitment of U.S. ground troops the next day.[94] The combat readiness of

MacArthur's Far East Command and South Korean troops was suddenly likely to be the foremost

concern on the collective mind of American political and military leadership.

Republic of Korea Army (ROKA) Readiness

When the U.S. troop withdrawal from South Korea began in September 1948, Congress

and the Truman administration debated over how to continue support to South Korea in the

absence of American troops. The options ranged from "an emphasis on economic assistance or on

---

[91]Leffler, *A Preponderance of Power*, 264-265.

[92]Converse III, *Rearming for the Cold War*, 137.

[93]Douglas Kinnard, *President Eisenhower and Strategy Management : A Study in Defense Politics* (Washington: Pergamon-Brassey's, 1989), 7.

[94]Schnabel, *Policy and Direction*, 79.

direct military aid."[95] The immediate plan was for departing U.S. units to transfer a substantial

quantity of small arms, bazookas, howitzers, ammunition, and vehicles to ROKA units. Because

the South Korean political leadership had clearly indicated an offensive mindset toward the North

Koreans in recent months, the U.S. intentionally withheld preemptive and expeditionary offensive

weapons, such as tanks and heavy artillery, from these transfers."[96] By contrast, the Soviet policy

on providing arms appeared far less concerned with limiting North Korean offensive capabilities,

as evidenced by the appearance of T-34 tanks in the early days of the war.[97] Because ROKA units

stored much of these supplies and equipment just south of the Thirty-eighth Parallel, the North

Korean army captured them as they crossed during the invasion.[98]

Concerning the longer-term approach to South Korean assistance, the debate between

Congress and the Administration over economic versus military assistance resulted in a plan to do

both. Congress eventually passed a measure to provide $30 million of economic assistance

through February 1950 while the mutual defense assistance program (MDAP), the path of direct

military assistance, would begin later in the year. The invasion, however, halted MDAP

assistance efforts just beginning in June 1950.[99]

Ultimately, as the war commenced in late June 1950, the South Korean Army consisted

of eight-divisions and 95,000 men—30,000 more than that which the United States had tailored

its KMAG and support plan.[100] Thus, significant shortages existed in equipment and KMAG

oversight capabilities. Meanwhile, the State Department and the CIA produced conflicting

estimates concerning the relative strength of North and South Korean armies just prior to the

---

[95]James A. Huston, *Outposts and Allies: U.S. Army Logistics in the Cold War, 1945-1953* (Selinsgrove: Susquehanna University Press, 1988), 226.

[96]Ibid., 225-226.

[97]Huston, *Guns and Butter, Powder and Rice*, 78; Huston, *Outposts and Allies*, 225.

[98]Huston, *Outposts and Allies*, 227.

[99]Ibid.

[100]Condit, *The Test of War*, 46.

North Korean invasion. U.S. Ambassador John Muccio estimated that ROK troops were at least equal to their northern counterparts in "training, leadership, morale, marksmanship and…small arms equipment" while the CIA noted that North Korean forces, possessing Soviet training, heavy armor, artillery and aircraft, could succeed in "short-term military operations against southern Korea, including the capture of Seoul."[101] Although both armies were in relative parity regarding overall troop strength, two ROKA divisions were consistently unable to train for conventional operations as they were deeply engaged in counterguerrilla operations in previous months.[102]

Far East Command (FECOM) Readiness

At the time of the North Korean invasion of South Korea, overall U.S. active duty troop strength was 38,000 troops less than its authorized 630,000, consisting of 591,000 troops organized in ten divisions, twelve separate regiments and forty-eight antiaircraft artillery battalions.[103] FECOM possessed 108,500 troops organized under the Eighth Army. The four divisions stationed in Japan represented the largest contingent of active duty American forces overseas.[104] The strength of active duty troops held in strategic reserve in the United States, contemporaneously referred to as the zone of the interior (ZI), was approximately 360,000 troops organized in five divisions.[105]

The four divisions assigned to the Eighth Army in Japan were the Seventh Infantry Division, the Twenty-Fourth Infantry Division, the Twenty-Fifth Infantry Division and the First Cavalry Division. All but the Twenty-Fifth were below their authorized peacetime strength of

---

[101]Ibid.

[102]Ibid.

[103]Converse III, *Rearming for the Cold War*, 138; Schnabel, *Policy and Direction*, 43, 45.

[104]Schnabel, *Policy and Direction*, 43.

[105]Ibid.

12,500 and all four were far below their authorized wartime strength of 18,900.[106] The result was that each division reconfigured its regiments to consist of only two, rather than the authorized three, battalions.[107] There were no tank companies and the division possessed only two-thirds of their artillery manpower and equipment requirements.[108] In sum, the actual strength of all Eighth Army combat troops in June 1950 was 49 percent of its wartime authorizations while the strength of its service troops dipped as low as 26 percent.[109]

Because peacetime materiel requirements, based almost entirely on leftover World War II stocks, appeared to be sufficient, active Army procurement during the interwar period "was limited mainly to food, clothing and medical supplies."[110] As compared to wartime authorizations, however, equipment shortages positioned each division as short 1,500 rifles, one hundred 90-mm anti-tank guns, three rifle battalions, six heavy tank companies, three 105-mm filed artillery battalions, and three antiaircraft artillery battalions.[111] Tank support consisted of division medium-tank battalions equipped only with M24 light tanks.[112] Put another way, Schnabel states: "In terms of battle potential, the infantry divisions could lay down only 62 percent of their infantry firepower, 69 percent of their antiaircraft artillery firepower, and 14 percent of their tank firepower."[113]

To address the equipment shortages and virtual lack of an active American military industrial base, FECOM activated an informal program in 1947, known as OPERATION ROLL-

[106]Charles E. Heller and William A. Stofft, *America's First Battles, 1776-1965* (Lawrence, KS: University Press of Kansas, 1986), 269.

[107]Ibid.

[108]Ibid.

[109]HQ Army Forces Far East and Eighth U.S. Army, "Logistics Study of the Korean Campaigns, 1950-1953, Vol I," (1954): 4.

[110]Schnabel, *Policy and Direction*, 45.

[111]Ibid., 54.

[112]Heller and Stofft, *America's First Battles*, 269.

[113]Schnabel, *Policy and Direction*, 54.

UP, that would remain FECOM's main source of supply in the years leading up to the war.[114] The intent of this program was to gather vehicles, signal equipment, armament and other war materiel left in place throughout the islands of the Far East at the end of World War II for re-issue to Eighth Army divisions.[115] Refurbishment of these items would employ revitalized FECOM "repair and rebuild facilities, including Japanese industry."[116] Overall, 75-90 percent of serviceable armament and automotive equipment held by the Eighth Army at the onset of the war was available solely because of ROLL-UP. Nonetheless, shortages of qualified personnel in the rebuild program meant much more equipment remained unserviceable, leaving the Eighth Army far short of its wartime requirements.[117]

In April 1949, General MacArthur, as the Commander in Chief, Far East Command (CINCFE), directed the establishment of a program that would create a "cohesive and integrated Naval, Air and Ground fighting team."[118] This directive reflected a change in the primary mission of all ground, naval and air forces in the Far East from guard and occupational duties to training for combat. This directive, however, was due less to any perception of a growing threat in the region as it was to recognition that Japan had achieved relatively stable internal political and economic conditions.[119]

For Army forces in Japan, the task of executing this training refocus fell directly to General Walton Walker, Commander of the U.S. Eighth Army. By June of 1950, Walker had progressed to the point where "all divisions of the Eighth Army had completed the battalion phase of training and had begun the regimental phase, with concurrent joint training" to include

---

[114]Ibid., 58.

[115]Ibid., 59.

[116]Ibid.

[117]Ibid.

[118]HQ, Army Forces Far East and Eighth U.S. Army, "Logistics Study of the Korean Campaigns," 17.

[119]Schnabel, *Policy and Direction*, 59-60.

an "active amphibious training program." [120] The ability to carry out larger-scale military training

exercises was constrained, however, because of limited training areas available at the time in a

highly populated, agriculturally based Japan.[121] The timing of the invasion of South Korea,

however, would make this largely irrelevant.

Despite grave shortages in equipment and personnel operating under a fledgling combat

training program, the most disconcerting element within FECOM at the onset of the war was the

strategic guidance under which it operated. With KMAG under the direction of the State

Department and all other troops withdrawn from Korea by July 1949, MacArthur's only

responsibility regarding Korea in June 1950 was "providing logistical support to the Korean

water line and being prepared to evacuate United States Nationals in the event of an

emergency."[122] A recommendation by the JCS to marginalize the strategic significance of Korea

led Truman to approve a policy in April 1948 stating "The United States should not become so

irrevocably involved in the Korean situation that an action taken by any faction in Korea *or by*

any other power in Korea could be considered a 'casus belli' for the United States."[123]

This sentiment towards Korea appeared to be publicly reaffirmed by Secretary of State

Dean Acheson in a January 1950 National Press Club address where "He acknowledged that in

time of *global war* the U.S. strategic defense perimeter was limited to Japan, Okinawa, and the

Philippines," clearly excluding South Korea.[124] Therefore, as late as January 1950, Truman,

Acheson and the JCS seemed to believe that if the Soviet Union wanted to establish full control

---

[120]HQ, Army Forces Far East and Eighth U.S. Army, "Logistics Study of the Korean Campaigns," 18.

[121]Schnabel, *Policy and Direction*, 55.

[122]HQ Army Forces Far East and Eighth U.S. Army, "Logistics Study of the Korean Campaigns," 3.

[123]Schnabel, *Policy and Direction*, 50 (italics added).The policy referenced here is the State-Army-Navy-Air Force Coordinating Committee (SANACC) policy 176/39, 22 March 1948, titled "U.S. Policy in Korea"

[124]Leffler, *A Preponderance of Power*, 338 (italics added).

over the Korean peninsula, the United States would not be in a military position to challenge them there.[125]

The Truman administration likely based their decision to respond to North Korean aggression with American force on the NSC 68 "limited war" approach to Communism developed in April 1950, just two months before the invasion and only three months after Acheson's Press Club address. Although the decision to enter this war conflicted with such previous policies and statements as mentioned above by the Truman administration regarding a "global war", it was in accordance with NSC 68 policy of "limited war." However, due to its development at only the NSC level by April 1950, such policy did not yet evolve into military planning guidance at the FECOM level or any other military command by June. Thus, due to the rapidly changing policies and consistently constrained budgets of the Truman administration regarding its military approach to Communism in the months leading up to the war, MacArthur and his staff unknowingly operated under obsolete guidance and with a woefully unprepared Army regarding upcoming events on the Korean peninsula.

The FY 1951 Military Budgets Supplementals

Although the Truman administration was likely concerned with the tactical readiness of American troops in Korea as the war began, in the larger perspective the Communist aggression there forced Truman to revise his cautious overall approach to rearmament. A review of FY 1951 military budget supplementals during the first six months of the war quantitatively reveals President Truman's changing views. It was a buildup not only geared for the situation in Korea, however, but any region perceived as "threatened by Communist aggression, particularly NATO Europe, Indochina and Formosa."[126] Although designed so as not to become a full mobilization on the scale of World War II, the scale of the effort marked significant changes in Truman's

---

[125]Schnabel, *Policy and Direction*, 50.

[126]Condit, *The Test of War*, 223.

policy. The primary concern with establishing an overly aggressive mobilization program was the risk of inducing such a massive influx of personnel that it would both quickly outpace the equipment available to those troops for training and combat, while simultaneously reducing the work force required by the industrial base to make such a mobilization possible.[127]

Prior to the onset of the war, Truman capped the FY 1951 military budget, which covered the fiscal year running from 1 July 1950 through 30 June 1951, at $13.4 billion, with roughly $4.11 billion appropriated for the Army, $4.09 billion for the Navy and $4.77 billion for the Air Force.[128] Total authorized force strength equaled 1.5 million: 630,000 for the Army; 461,000 for the Navy and Marines; and 416,000 for the Air Force. On 19 July 1950, Truman authorized an increase in total Army strength to 843,000, with a corresponding $3.1 billion supplemental to the Army budget. Truman further increased the Army endstrength to 1.35 million by 14 December with a second corresponding supplemental request of $9.2 billion.[129] By 30 June 1951, with the addition of yet another supplemental and corresponding increase in authorized strength in May 1951, the Army would attain its new goal of 1.5 million troops, eighteen divisions, eighteen separate regiments and 103 separate antiaircraft artillery battalions.[130]

The supplemental of December 1950 mentioned above, influenced by the suspected intervention of Chinese forces in November, directed $4.5 billion of the Army's $9.2 billion authorization towards equipment procurement.[131] The amount of money appropriated by this one supplemental nearly equaled the combined $5 billion appropriated for Army procurement in both FY 1949 and FY 1950, most of which was spent on "food, clothing, and other basic supplies" and

---

[127]Huston, *Guns and Butter, Powder and Rice*, 108-109.

[128]Rearden, *The Formative Years*, 380.

[129]Condit, *The Test of War*, 238.

[130]Ibid.

[131]Ibid., 236-237.

"materiel for other government agencies."[132] Likewise, the Army research and development budget for FY 1951 increased to over $300 million, nearly three times the amount appropriated the previous year.[133] Thus, in response to the ground war in Korea, military funding for procurement and RDT&E, which swayed strongly towards air power and the Air Force in particular during the interwar years, was reappearing in the Army budget.

American Industrial Support, Strategic Sustainment and a National Emergency

Constrained budgets and the "fragmented structure" of the Army organizations focused on research, development and procurement during the World War II-Korea interwar period steered these Army programs into a nebulous and undeveloped condition.[134] Accordingly, the industrial base potentially available to support these Army programs focused on civilian economic opportunities instead. Thus, the rapid influx of money into military budgets throughout the fall and winter of 1950 could not readily overcome the inertia of a dormant industrial base and provide immediate materiel solutions to requirements in Korea.[135]

Considering its lean budgetary circumstances during the World War II-Korea interwar years, the Army had made impressive, albeit modest, efforts to design and procure trucks, antiaircraft systems, and upgraded light, medium and heavy tanks.[136] A relatively inactive industrial base and fledgling coordinating government agencies, however, could not quickly provide such items in the quantities suddenly required by the outbreak of war.[137] The critical first six months of the war would find the Army in Korea relying almost entirely on the World War II

---

[132]Converse III, *Rearming for the Cold War*, 171.

[133]Ibid., 156.

[134]Ibid., 137-138.

[135]Ibid., 138.

[136]Ibid., 171-173.

[137]Ibid., 173.

stocks of the Far East and stateside inventories as General Larkin predicted three weeks before the invasion.[138]

The foremost element that initially confounded Army sustainment planners regarding the war in Korea was deriving guidance on the extent of mobilization. A lack of operational contingency planning in the Far East Command Theater before the war created a void on how to visualize sustainment efforts. A meeting of the Army staff in mid-July 1950 concluded with a consensus by the Army G-1, G-3 and G-4 that "definite planning goals must be established for all aspects of the Army's expansion as soon as possible" and the Army G-4 described the overall supply program for support to the war effort as "hand-to-mouth."[139] Thus, one the of more unexpected, yet complex, problems inherent to sustainment planning for an unplanned "limited" versus "total" war triggered during a low point in Army readiness is determining the "level of mobilization to be sought."[140] Further confounding the specific situation in Korea, Army logistics planners would soon find themselves having to consider requirements for U.S. Marine and ROK divisions, U.S. airmen, and "supplemental support for ground forces provided by other members of the United Nations."[141]

Excluding troops, one of the most urgent requirements identified in the first weeks of the war was the need for more howitzer and mortar ammunition. FECOM sustainment planners based their Class V stockages in Japan on reduced strength divisions operating under peacetime conditions. The changes in requirements were considerable. By mid-July, for example, the "ammunition required to support one infantry division for one day" changed from 147 tons to 553 tons.[142] A dormant industrial base forced the Army to supply nearly all ammunition requirements

---

[138]Huston, *Guns and Butter, Powder and Rice*, 171.

[139]Schnabel, *Policy and Direction*, 118.

[140]Huston, *Guns and Butter, Powder and Rice*, 94.

[141]Ibid.

[142]Ibid., 77.

with World War II stocks. For example, Huston notes that by the end of November 1950 "105-mm howitzers alone had fired over 1,250,000 rounds of ammunition in Korea. Three times that much had arrived at the theater—and none of this ammunition had been produced since 1945."[143] Despite the extensive age of most of the ammunition provided during the early months of the war, it generally performed to standard and without malfunction.[144] However, the shipment of most global stockages of ammunition to the Korean theater without resupply by the industrial base placed U.S. units in other regions of the world at an increased level of risk.

A shortage of American medium tanks and antitank weapons also presented an immediate challenge with the early involvement of Soviet tanks, primarily T-34s, in the war on the side of North Korea. The newly developed antitank 3.5-inch rocket launcher, of limited but immediate availability in Korea, proved effective by destroying seven enemy tanks on one day alone in July.[145] In this specific case, the industrial base elements supplying this weapon, now empowered by the budget procurement supplemental of July, were able to deliver 40,000 3.5-inch rockets to Korea by the end of August and "virtually" meet the demand within a month.[146]

Because stockages in Japan offered light tanks almost exclusively, units and depots in the U.S. shipped over 1,100 medium tanks, of four different models, to Korea by 1 October 1950. Two hundred of these included the M-46 Patton, which proved the most commensurate to the T-34 threat.[147] Huston notes "In one major engagement, sixteen M-46 Pattons were reported to have knocked out eighteen Communist T-34s and a self-propelled gun at a cost of only four slightly damaged American tanks."[148] However, the age and various models of the tanks, combined with a

---

[143]Ibid., 102.

[144]Ibid., 170.

[145]Ibid., 78.

[146]Ibid., 90.

[147]Ibid., 175-176.

[148]Ibid., 177.

lack of qualified maintenance units, would confound the supply system and plague the operational readiness rates of these tanks until heavy ordnance companies arrived in Korea in 1951.[149]

In early December, General Larkin devised an emergency plan to coordinate a massive shipment of equipment soon headed for Korea.[150] Spurred by MacArthur's rapid spike in troop and materiel requests as Chinese attacks began to punish Eighth Army troops, the plan, code-named OPERATION PINK, was to combat load an entire division's worth of essential equipment, minus ammunition, into eight ships for rapid deployment directly to Korea.[151] With equipment arriving at ports in Seattle and San Francisco from depots in St. Louis, Chicago, New York, Philadelphia and Baltimore, the shipments set sail for Korea on 9 December, less than five days after Larkin ordered the plan to commence.[152] Such experiences would serve as blueprints for Army sustainment planners to expedite future emergency requests throughout the war.[153]

Although reports from Korea confirmed the presence of Chinese combat forces there by mid-December 1950, it was the desire to create "a military posture and a mobilization base" from which, if necessary, it would be possible to launch a global war against Communism that spurred President Truman to declare a state of national emergency on 16 December 1950.[154] As a corollary to this decision, Truman established the Office of Defense Mobilization under Charles E. Wilson, the president of the General Electric Company, to streamline the national mobilization effort.[155] In support of the effort, Truman pushed again to increase military funding which

---

[149]Arthur W. Conner Jr., "The Armor Debacle in Korea, 1950: Implications for Today," *Parameters*, (Summer 1992): 73-74.

[150]Huston, *Guns and Butter, Powder and Rice*, 106.

[151]Schnabel, *Policy and Direction*, 297.

[152]Huston, *Guns and Butter, Powder and Rice*, 107.

[153]Ibid., 108.

[154]Leffler, *A Preponderance of Power*, 402-403.

[155]Ibid., 403.

resulted in yet another FY 1951 supplemental, the fourth, which provided another $6.38 billion, approved by Congress on 31 May 1951.[156]

Specifically concerning the increases in Army budgeting for research and development throughout the entire Korean War, Elliot Converse III writes "The three fiscal years spanning the Korean War were a period of relative plenty for Army research and development – a total of $1.14 billion appropriated for FY 1951-1953 against $469 million for the four fiscal years from 1947 through 1950."[157] However, Army Research and Development Program directors focused these funds more towards "possible ground combat in Europe," presumably against a numerically superior Soviet force, than for actual fighting conditions in Korea.[158]

Regarding procurement, Converse notes "From FY 1948 through FY 1950, procurement funds available to the Army amounted to approximately $5 billion. In sharp contrast, during the period of war and rearmament from FY 1951 through 1953, the Army received $19.6 billion for procurement, or about 27 percent of the total of $72 billion that Congress appropriated for all military procurement."[159] By the end of the war, Army procurement efforts would result in having nearly 12,000 tanks, 105,000 .50-caliber machine guns, and 115,000 two and one-half ton trucks purchased and delivered to its stocks.[160] Total Army personnel authorizations from FY 1951-1953 would hover between 1.5 and 1.6 million troops.[161] It seemed that President Truman had turned the page to a new chapter in American history regarding the relationship between its military and its industrial base.

---

[156]Condit, *The Test of War*, 240.

[157]Converse III, *Rearming for the Cold War*, 157.

[158]Ibid., 156-157.

[159]Ibid., 170.

[160]Ibid.

[161]Condit, *The Test of War*, 255, 278.

The transition of the presidency from Harry S. Truman to Dwight D. Eisenhower in January 1953 brought into that office different views regarding the interdependency between domestic economy, foreign policy, defense spending and national security. Regarding national security strategy, Eisenhower further challenged the fundamental principles of deterrence that steered policy and action in the previous administration. From the outset of his presidency, Eisenhower sought predictable and balanced spending in both defense and domestic programs while establishing and maintaining the strategic initiative against a communist coalition of nations, led by the Soviet Union.

In mid-December 1952, over a month *before* his inauguration, president-elect Dwight D. Eisenhower wasted no time sending intentionally ambiguous messages, or, perhaps more appropriately, veiled threats, towards the patrons of communist force in the ongoing Korean War - China and the Soviet Union. Earlier that month, Eisenhower, in the fulfillment of a campaign promise, spent three days personally inspecting the military conditions on the ground throughout Korea.[162] Following this tour, he flew from Seoul to Guam and, from there, embarked on a ten-day cruise with several members of what would become his future Cabinet aboard the USS *Helena*, and arrived at Pearl Harbor on 14 December 1952.[163] Here Eisenhower revealed to the press his views regarding the Korean situation, "We face an enemy whom we cannot hope to impress by words, however eloquent, but only by deeds—executed under circumstances of our choosing."[164]

Although this statement specifically reflected Eisenhower's view towards the strategic situation in Korea as of December 1952, it is a comment strikingly similar to that made over a

---

[162]Jean Edward Smith, *Eisenhower: In War and Peace* (New York: Random House, 2012), 557-560.

[163]Ibid., 561.

[164]Ibid.

year later by his Secretary of State, John Foster Dulles, regarding the administration's overall approach to a new national security strategy. Speaking before the members of Council of Foreign Relations in January 1954, Dulles stated, "The way to deter aggression is for a free community to be willing and able to respond vigorously and at places and with means of its own choosing. The basic decision was [made] to depend primarily on a great capacity to retaliate, instantly, by means and at places of our choosing."[165] Dulles' comment, unlike that of Eisenhower made a year before, would illicit "rapid, intense and largely critical" national and international reaction.[166] The sentiment thinly veiled in both statements is that United States exclusively possesses the global strategic military initiative and the will to exercise it. This sentiment, soon known as the "Massive Retaliation" policy, represented a major pillar in the overall strategic framework developed by the Eisenhower administration throughout 1953, a framework it referred to as the "New Look."[167] This section explores how the New Look came to be, how it would evolve over Eisenhower's eight years in office, and how this approach would affect both the military and the American industrial base.

Eisenhower's Vision

Much like many of his previous command positions in the military, Eisenhower came into the office of the Presidency with an approach designed to transform current conditions into those he considered more desirable. However, the methods available to President Eisenhower in conducting this transformation were far more diffuse and, therefore, more challenging than those available to General Eisenhower, even for the man who once steered the enormous Operation Overlord and the subsequent drive of Allied forces across Western Europe less than ten years

---

[165]Kinnard, *President Eisenhower and Strategy Management*, 27.

[166]Robert R. Bowie and Richard H. Immerman, *Waging Peace : How Eisenhower Shaped an Enduring Cold War Strategy* (New York: Oxford University Press, 1998), 199; Kinnard, *President Eisenhower and Strategy Management*, 27.

[167]Bowie and Immerman, *Waging Peace*, 24, 200; House, *A Military History of the Cold War, 1944-1962*, 224.

earlier. Regardless, his overall vision, as expressed to his future Cabinet while aboard the USS *Helena* in December 1952 was clear: end the Korean War, balance the budget, and reduce taxes while continuing many of New Deal social programs.[168] Eisenhower expressed his view on the proverbial "guns versus butter" tension more emotionally while drafting his formal response to the death of Joseph Stalin in March 1953. While preparing the speech, Eisenhower told his speechwriter, Emmet Hughes, that, "he wanted to see the resources of the world used for bread, clothes, homes, hospitals and schools, but not for guns."[169]

In fact, all of these objectives—ending the Korean War, balancing the budget, reducing taxes, and maintaining an adequate defense—were interrelated.[170] In order to reduce spending and balance the budget, the war in Korea had to end. President Truman's FY1954 budget "requested new appropriations totaling $72.9 billion, of which the Defense Department's share was $41.3 billion, almost 57 percent" and would add nearly $10 billion to the national debt.[171] Therefore, as a starting point for tackling the budget issue, Eisenhower viewed an end to the war as the doorway to responsible reduction in military spending, thus reducing overall expenditures and paving the way for a balanced budget. A balanced budget and decreased expenditures could then permit a reduction in taxes. By 1 August 1953, six months into his presidency, Eisenhower would announce both the signing of an armistice in Korea and the reduction of the FY1954 military budget submitted by the Truman administration by more than $6 billion. In the next twelve months, although not yet able to balance the budget, he was able to reduce taxes.[172]

Eisenhower did not create national security strategy in a vacuum. Like all presidents, his initial groundwork in this area had its links to the previous administration. While agreeing with

[168]Smith, *Eisenhower*, 560.

[169]Ibid., 573.

[170]Kinnard, *President Eisenhower and Strategy Management*, 36.

[171]Richard M. Leighton, *Strategy, Money, and the New Look, 1953-1956* (Washington, DC.: Historical Office, Office of the Secretary of Defense, 2001), 65-66.

[172]Kinnard, *President Eisenhower and Strategy Management*, 36.

the policy of containment, Eisenhower fundamentally rejected the concept of "the year of maximum danger" that drove the national security strategy of the Truman administration since 1950.[173] This concept, developed during the study that helped to formulate NSC-68, specifically asserted that, "the USSR would have sufficient atomic bombs and means of delivery to offset significantly the U.S. nuclear capability" by 1954, making it the "crisis year."[174] The fear was not so much "purposeful Soviet military aggression" but the diplomatic power afforded to them by such a position.[175] If the USSR attained nuclear parity with the United States, the study proposed, "America's allies might refrain from joining this country in taking a more positive political position against the USSR."[176]

For his part, Eisenhower believed that the Soviet threat would exist indefinitely and consequently viewed the necessary approach not as one revolving around a fixed point in time, but for the "long haul."[177] In April 1953, Eisenhower expressed this view at a press conference by stating, "Defense is not a matter of maximum strength for a single date."[178] Thus, Eisenhower reasoned, strategic policy and budget must accord and accommodate military strength in a level, predictable way. He was critical of Truman's rapid demobilization processes following World War II and subsequent withdrawal from Korea, both of which he felt invited attack.[179] He was further critical of the sudden quadrupling of defense expenditures following the onset of the

---

[173]Bowie and Immerman, *Waging Peace*, 5, 106, 153; Kinnard, *President Eisenhower and Strategy Management*, 8.

[174]Kinnard, *President Eisenhower and Strategy Management*, 6-8; Bowie and Immerman, *Waging Peace*, 17, 153.

[175]Leffler, *A Preponderance of Power*, 332.

[176]Ibid., 333.

[177]Bowie and Immerman, *Waging Peace*, 5, 40, 96; Kinnard, *President Eisenhower and Strategy Management*, 8.

[178]United States National Archives, *The Public Papers of the President, Dwight D. Eisenhower, 1953* (Washington DC: U.S. Government Printing Office, 1960), 242; Kinnard, *President Eisenhower and Strategy Management*, 8.

[179]Smith, *Eisenhower*, 639.

Korean War.[180] In order to minimize "economic dislocation," Eisenhower wanted to avoid such "alternative buildups and drops in military expenditures."[181]

The question then was how could the United States retain the global strategic military initiative relative to the Soviet Union while programming defense spending in a sustainable and predictable way? The answer, as Eisenhower summarized it in his memoirs following his years in the White House, was to relax the assumption that "America's response to attack would have to accord with the exact nature of aggression. For example, an invasion of Europe in overwhelming strength by conventional forces did not mean that our reaction had to be limited to force of the same kind."[182] Or, put another way, as stated by Eisenhower's Vice President, Richard Nixon, "Rather than let the Communists nibble us to death all over the world in little wars, we would rely in the future primarily on our massive mobile retaliation power…against the major source of aggression."[183] In other words, the United States would stop the expensive practice of matching communist forces "division for division" wherever they may appear. In its most extreme form, one could interpret the policy as one in which the United States would respond to even limited communist aggression at any point on the globe with a nuclear attack on Moscow—the presumable "source" of aggression. Hence, the United States would no longer react to the whims of communist behavior, and consequently retain the strategic initiative for itself. Thus, Eisenhower did not disregard Truman's policy of containment, only the manner in which he executed it. The next section of this paper examines Eisenhower's views on containment, as articulated in the New Look, translated into a national military strategy and force structure throughout his eight years as president.

---

[180]Ibid.

[181]Kinnard, *President Eisenhower and Strategy Management*, 8.

[182]Dwight D. Eisenhower, *The White House Years (Volume 1): Mandate for Change, 1953-1956* (Garden City, NY: Doubleday, 1963), 446; Kinnard, *President Eisenhower and Strategy Management*, 9.

[183]Smith, *Eisenhower*, 644.

In his efforts to avoid major combat operations while retaining a position of relative advantage in the Cold War, Eisenhower complemented his policy of massive retaliation with that of extensive covert operations and psychological warfare. In fact, one could argue that the concept of massive retaliation itself was indeed psychological warfare at its zenith. Even during his campaign in October 1952, Eisenhower openly declared the importance of psychological warfare and "Blasted the Truman administration for neglecting this important dimension of the Cold War struggle...and went on to promise that, if elected, he would make psychological warfare a central focus of U.S. national security strategy."[184] Regarding covert operations, Eisenhower approved Operations AJAX and PBSUCCSESS, two Central Intelligence Agency (CIA)-directed coups in Iran and Guatemala, respectively, in his first eighteen months in office.[185] In fact, Eisenhower intended both coups to disrupt suspected communist influence within and around those countries and began to view the CIA as an alternate "quick fix" approach to foreign policy problems relative to the Cold War.[186] The focus of this monograph, however, rests with the views of the Truman and Eisenhower administrations towards conventional military force and the effect of their policies on force structure and the national industrial base.

The New Look and Two Army Chiefs: A Philosophical Clash

In the months following his massive retaliation-themed address to the Council of Foreign Affairs in January 1954, Dulles himself attempted to soften the perceived hard line sentiment by publishing a more expansive and systematic explanation of the New Look approach in the April 1954 issue of *Foreign Affairs*.[187] Admiral Arthur Radford, the Chairman of the Joint Chiefs, also attempted to clarify the concept more thoroughly at a press conference in March. Radford stated,

---

[184]Kenneth Alan Osgood, *Total Cold War: Eisenhower's Secret Propaganda Battle at Home and Abroad* (Lawrence, KS: University of Kansas, 2006), 46.

[185]Smith, *Eisenhower*, 617-633.

[186]Ibid., 627.

[187]Leighton, *Strategy, Money, and the New Look*, 226.

"It is not correct to say that we are relying exclusively on one weapon, or one service, or that we are anticipating one kind of war. I believe that this Nation could be a prisoner of its own military posture if it had no capability, other than to deliver a massive atomic attack…It certainly should be evident from the forces we intend to maintain that we are not relying solely on air power."[188] Radford further clarified by explaining that the combination of this air power, specifically nuclear-capable bombers, with a "million-man Army and the most powerful Navy in the world," afforded the administration the capability to approach communist aggression in an intentionally ambiguous manner, designed specifically to "keep them guessing."[189] As Leighton notes, despite these and other attempts to enlighten the public on the breadth and pragmatic foundations of Eisenhower's national security policy, "In the popular mind…massive retaliation was to become virtually synonymous with the New Look."[190]

The nature of the New Look appeared ambiguous enough to leave even the service chiefs guessing as to how to align their force structures with such an approach. Nevertheless, with a strategy at least outlined and presented to the public by the summer of 1954, the next steps of the administration were to incorporate these ideas into a formal plan circumscribed by the fiscal promises of the President. Although Radford's description mentioned above certainly sounded like a balanced-force approach, fiscal constraints and directives based on Executive and Congressional preferences regarding force composition would force the Army, in particular, to suffer.

General Matthew Ridgway spent his tenure as the Army Chief of Staff from 1953 through 1955 opposed to the overall concept of the New Look.[191] Specifically, he opposed the

---

[188]Ibid., 224.

[189]Ibid.

[190]Ibid., 228-229.

[191]For an excellent summary of General Ridgway's opposition and responses to Eisenhower's Basic National Security Policy, see: Andrew J. Bacevich, "The Paradox of Professionalism: Eisenhower, Ridgway, and the Challange to Civilian Control, 1953-1955," *The Journal of Military History* 61, no. 2

effects of the approach on Army structure and disposition while being implemented. Regarding ground forces, the New Look concept ultimately would come to propose that Army forces concentrate in the United States and serve as "mobile central reserves" while the "first response to limited aggression anywhere would be by whatever allied forces were immediately involved."[192] The budgetary considerations of this concept implied "the large-scale withdrawal of U.S. forces from overseas and an overall reduction in uniformed manpower," actions that would diminish the strategic role of the Army overseas and substituting them with allied ground forces.[193]

Ridgway even doubted the administration's intention of using the Army as a "mobile central reserve" because the Air Force continued to dilute its troop carrying capacity in favor of bombers.[194] It is a suspicion perhaps borne out by Eisenhower himself in a comment he made later to the next Army Chief of Staff, General Maxwell Taylor. At a White House meeting in May 1956, Eisenhower indicated to Taylor that, in his view, the Army's role in a future war, presumably nuclear, would be to "maintain order at home."[195]

Despite his objections to strategic troop withdrawal and overall force reductions, Ridgway's primary concern was that massive retaliation was steering the military toward what he felt was an unrealistic view toward future wars.[196] To this end, Ridgway commented, "Wars are still fought for little bits of bloody earth, and they are only ended when the enemy's will to resist

---

(April 1997); For a more detailed examination of this topic, see Chapters 30 through 38 of: Matthew B. Ridgway and Harold H. Martin, *Soldier: The Memoirs of Matthew B. Ridgway* (New York: Harper, 1956).

[192]Leighton, *Strategy, Money, and the New Look*, 193, 224.

[193]Ibid., 193.

[194]Ridgway and Martin, *Soldier*, 312-316; Bart Howard, "Army Transformation, 1953-1961: Lessons of the "New Look" Army" (U.S. Army War College - Army Heritage Collection Online, 2004), 5.

[195]Converse III, *Rearming for the Cold War*, 595-596.

[196]Ridgway and Martin, *Soldier*, 273.

is broken, and armed men stand victorious on his home soil."[197] In June 1955, after serving only two years as Army Chief of Staff, Ridgway "retired in frustration."[198]

Ridgway's replacement as Army Chief of Staff was General Maxwell Taylor. Although Taylor's political skill persuaded the administration to view him as more palatable than Ridgway, he quickly made known his fundamental objections to the New Look and ultimately earned himself "a reputation as a dissenter" within the JCS.[199] Taylor's objections were almost identical to those of Ridgway but now made more credible as the Soviet nuclear arsenal presumably approached parity with the United States. In a meeting of the Joint Chiefs in July 1956, Taylor commented that the planned reductions in overall Army endstrength and the withdrawal of U.S. troops from Europe and Asia both represent "a program which prepares for one improbable type of war, while leaving the United States weak in its ability to meet the most probable type of threat."[200] Throughout the spring and summer of 1956, Taylor reasoned that if both the Soviet Union and the United States possessed an equal nuclear capability, "any war was likely to be a small one."[201] Accordingly, strategic nuclear capabilities would become "sterile assets" and that "small atomic task forces...cannot substitute for forces [eliminated in the plan] able to seize and hold ground."[202] In short, Taylor was implying that the New Look strategy was driven mostly by politics and concerns for the domestic economy. For Taylor it went too far in substituting atomic for conventional force, and ignored the likely nature of future wars at the peril of true security.

---

[197]Ibid., 290.

[198]Howard, "Army Transformation, 1953-1961", 7.

[199]Robert J. Watson, *Into the Missile Age, 1956-1960* (Washington, DC: Historical Office, Office of the Secretary of Defense, 1997), 22; Howard, "Army Transformation, 1953-1961", 11; For a detailed account of General's Taylor's opposition to Eisenhower's Basic National Security Policy, see: Maxwell D. Taylor, *The Uncertain Trumpet* (New York: Harper, 1960).

[200]Taylor, *The Uncertain Trumpet*, 40-41.

[201]Kinnard, *President Eisenhower and Strategy Management*, 55.

[202]Leighton, *Strategy, Money, and the New Look*, 665.

Despite his objections and "reputation as a dissenter," however, Taylor did serve as the Army Chief of Staff for four years before retiring (the first time) in 1959.[203]

Merging the New Look, the Army and the Industrial Base

Despite their philosophical objections to the New Look, both Ridgway and Taylor worked vigorously to accommodate the approach. Ridgway oversaw significant endstrength and budgets reductions while Taylor implemented radical changes to the Army force structure.[204] During Ridgway's tenure from the summer of 1953 through 1955, the Army shrank over 25 percent from over 1.5 million troops to 1.1 million.[205] With respect to the total defense force, these cuts would reduce the Army from 44 percent to 38 percent of the whole, while Air Force strength actually increased from 27 percent to 32 percent.[206]

Despite these reductions in force, however, Ridgway boasted that the incorporation of technology made it more lethal. For example, he noted that modern infantry division, while comparable in size to those of World War II, could generate 84 percent greater firepower.[207] Regarding the fiscal situation under Ridgway, the Army's budget for FY1955 was $7.6 billion, $5.3 billion less than FY1954.[208] By comparison, the Air Force FY1955 budget shrank only $349 million from FY1954 while the Navy budget actually increased $274 million.[209] Viewed as a whole, the Army drew almost 38 percent of the total defense budget in FY1954, dropping to 26 percent in FY1955.

[203]Smith, *Eisenhower*, 645; Watson, *Into the Missile Age*, 22.

[204]Howard, "Army Transformation, 1953-1961", 7; Robert T. Davis II, *The Challenge of Adaptation: The US Army in the Aftermath of Conflict, 1953 - 2000* (Fort Leavenworth, KS: Combat Studies Institute Press, 2008), 24.

[205]Leighton, *Strategy, Money, and the New Look*, 180; U.S. Dept. of Defense, *National Defense Budget Estimates for FY 2000*, 208.

[206]Leighton, *Strategy, Money, and the New Look*, 180.

[207]Ibid., 247.

[208]Ibid., 251.

[209]Ibid., 113, 254.

Under Taylor, similar trends would continue. From FY1955 through FY1961, the total active force endstrength would drop from 1.1 million troops to 883,000 with a corresponding drop from nineteen to fifteen divisions.[210] During this same period, Converse notes, "[the Army] received the smallest share of the budget, averaging about 23 percent to the Navy's nearly 30 percent and the Air Force's just over 44 percent."[211]

However, General Taylor's most innovative and controversial contribution to the Army during his tenure was the implementation of the Pentomic Division. The Pentomic Division concept fell out of an Army War College study dubbed PENTANA (pentagonal atomic-nonatomic army) initiated by Ridgway and other army leaders in 1954 who held the belief "that the psychology of something new and atomic would assist [the Army] in this budget battle."[212] As the name of the study implies, the goal was to develop a "dual-capable" force, or one capable of fighting by either atomic or conventional means.[213] As the name further implies, the Pentomic Division would consist of five battle groups with atomic capabilities, eliminating the regiment.[214] In accordance with Eisenhower's directive to Taylor for smaller divisions, the Pentomic infantry division highlighted a significant reduction in endstrength, from 17,000 to fewer than 14,000 men (with airborne divisions reduced to fewer than 12,000 men) with corresponding reductions in tanks, armored personnel carriers, and heavy artillery.[215]

Also under the tenures of both Ridgway and Taylor began the extensive and inextricable meshing of the defense industry and the Army so apparent today. The impetus for this relationship was the Army's zeal for rocket and guided missile development felt to be of such

[210]Converse III, *Rearming for the Cold War*, 594-595.

[211]Ibid., 594.

[212]Kinnard, *President Eisenhower and Strategy Management*, 58.

[213]Ibid; Davis II, *The Challenge of Adaptation*, 25.

[214]Kinnard, *President Eisenhower and Strategy Management*, 58; Howard, "Army Transformation, 1953-1961", 11; Davis II, *The Challenge of Adaptation*, 26.

[215]Davis II, *The Challenge of Adaptation*, 23, 26.

importance to its budgetary survival and operational relevance at the time. Driven initially as a means to "extend artillery" and deliver atomic or conventional warheads across the enlarged battlefields of the atomic age, the need for missiles also fit nicely into the Army's primary role under the New Look, homeland air defense. Improved missile technology also addressed the long-standing Army concern regarding insufficient close air support because of an institutional bias in the Air Force towards strategic bombing.[216] The Army's pursuit of rocket and missile technology quickly escalated and peaked in January 1958 with the launching of a Jupiter rocket (Juno I) that successfully placed the first American satellite (Explorer I) into orbit.[217] In retrospect, it was an ironic endeavor. As Converse notes, "at the same time it embraced nuclear systems, the Army rejected the national security strategy that relied on them."[218] In fact, the Army often times led the services in their development during this period.[219] For example, by 1955 the Army was managing nine separate missile systems intended for space exploration, tactical surface-to-surface, and air defense purposes.[220]

Throughout the 1950s, Redstone Arsenal, Alabama grew to become the center for Army rocket and missile development.[221] The prime organization behind this effort was the Guided Missile Development Division, Ordnance Missile Laboratory, which initially consisted of a mixture of several hundred U.S. civilian and military engineers, in addition to over 100 German scientists.[222] The German scientists were brought to the United States immediately following

---

[216]Converse III, *Rearming for the Cold War*, 596, 601; Howard, "Army Transformation, 1953-1961", 8.

[217]Watson, *Into the Missile Age*, 187; Converse III, *Rearming for the Cold War*, 592.

[218]Converse III, *Rearming for the Cold War*, 594.

[219]Eisenhower, *Mandate for Change*, 456.

[220]Howard, "Army Transformation, 1953-1961", 8.

[221]Erik Bergaust, *Rocket City, U.S.A.: From Huntsville, Alabama to the Moon* (New York: Macmillan, 1963), 65.

[222]David S. Akens, *Historical Origins of the George C. Marshall Space Flight Center.* (Huntsville, AL: Historical Office, Office of Management Services, George C. Marshall Space Flight Center, National Aeronautics and Space Administration, 1960), 36-38.

World War II in Europe under the direction Project Paperclip, an operation tied to harnessing the advances of the German scientific community under the Nazi regime for specific U.S. military purposes. [223]

In February 1956, this organization fell under the control of the new Army Ballistic Missile Agency (ABMA).[224] The primary purpose of this agency was the research and development of the Redstone Missile Program and the Intermediate Range Ballistic Missile [IRBM] Program (with the Army IRBM soon dubbed as the Jupiter missile).[225] The first commanding general of ABMA, Major General John Medaris, was adamant in retaining Army control in development of Jupiter by using the "arsenal concept."[226] Under this concept, Army civilians and soldiers would maintain the technical competence and project involvement to ensure complete oversight and management of a missile program and not be "technically at the mercy" of contractors.[227] Medaris' concern was that industry, if given full control of the process, would more freely implement priorities mandated by shareholders, priorities that may not always align with those of the warfighter.[228] However, even though Guided Missile Development Division grew to almost 3,000 personnel by the end of 1956, the requirements for accelerated progress forced Medaris to recognize the need for greater industry involvement during development.[229] As a result, Medaris, who selected the Chrysler Corporation for the production of Jupiter (the same company to produce the Redstone missile), authorized twenty-six Chrysler engineers to work

---

[223]Clarence G. Lasby, *Project Paperclip: German Scientists and the Cold War* (New York: Atheneum, 1971), 154-155.

[224]Akens, *Historical Origins of the George C. Marshall Space Flight Center*, 37-38, 41; Converse III, Rearming for the Cold War, 620-623.

[225]Akens, *Historical Origins of the George C. Marshall Space Flight Center*, 42.

[226]Converse III, *Rearming for the Cold War*, 623.

[227]John B. Medaris, *Countdown for Decision* (New York: Putnam, 1960), 99.

[228]Converse III, *Rearming for the Cold War*, 623.

[229]Ibid., 625.

directly with von Braun's team, a number that eventually grew to 650.[230] Further, to support its own efforts on the Redstone and Jupiter projects from October 1956 through August 1958, Chrysler "employed over 2,400 subcontractors and suppliers."[231] Outside of Chrysler, other production subcontractors working closely with Medaris' team on the development of Jupiter's engine, guidance and control assemblies, and reentry vehicle were the Rocketdyne Division of North American Aviation, the Ford Instrument Division of the Sperry Rand Corporation, and the Goodyear Aircraft Corporation, respectively.[232]

Thus, although Converse argued that the Army maintained strict control of the Jupiter program, the influence that industry came to exert directly on the effort over time is difficult not to notice. It becomes even more difficult to imagine how one would untangle such a deeply interwoven military-industrial relationship, especially considering that Jupiter was only one of many such extensive missile programs. According to General Taylor, the costs associated with such endeavors became the "primary concern" of the Defense Department during the Eisenhower presidency after the summer of 1956.[233] In addition, despite Medaris' concerns regarding the loss of technical competence and control of missile programs by the civilian and military members of the Army, the "arsenal concept" increasingly gave way to greater industry-based project management by the end of the decade.[234]

Conclusions Regarding the Eisenhower Era, Military Budgets and the Industrial Base

At the outset of his presidency, Eisenhower sought to establish and maintain a fiscal balance between defense spending and domestic programs with an overall reduction in taxes and

---

[230]Ibid., 626.

[231]Ibid.

[232]Ibid., 624-625.

[233]Taylor, *The Uncertain Trumpet*, 47.

[234]Converse III, *Rearming for the Cold War*, 633.

federal expenditures.[235] He believed that by ending hostilities in Korea and shifting national strategy within the rubric of the New Look, national security would become both strong and affordable. More specifically, Eisenhower sought a defense-spending pattern that was predictable and level, not subject to sizeable "knee-jerk" responses to perceived strategic threats.[236] Controlled and consistent defense spending would help facilitate what Eisenhower perceived as the true key to national security—a strong economy.

A review of the Eisenhower military budgets of FY1953 through FY1960 reveals that he accomplished his goal of relatively stable defense spending (Figure 1). One may also notice that defense spending in the years following the Korean War, although more stable, rested at a general baseline much higher than before the war period. A previous Secretary of Defense, George C. Marshall, initially envisioned a "higher plateau" concept that the Eisenhower administration adopted and implemented.[237] Marshall essentially linked the concept of a "higher plateau" of defense spending to an increased state of readiness, one he termed "limited mobilization." Marshall stated, "This is not full mobilization. This is a raising up of the whole establishment to gain momentum from which we can open the throttle and go very quickly in any required direction." Once reached, the plateau "would be one that might be maintained indefinitely, if necessary, without becoming a damaging economic burden."[238] In short, Marshall recognized the increasing international responsibilities of the United States in the longer term and applying a

---

[235]Smith, *Eisenhower*, 560.

[236]Bowie and Immerman, *Waging Peace*, 75.

[237]Leighton, *Strategy, Money, and the New Look*, 95.

[238]Ibid.

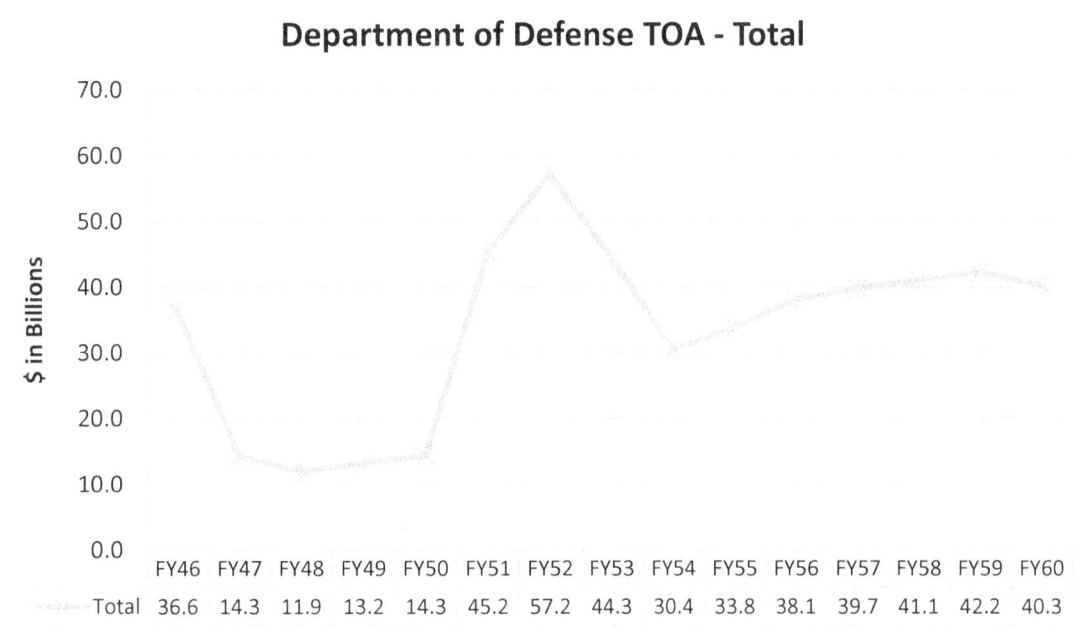

Department of Defense TOA - Total

	FY46	FY47	FY48	FY49	FY50	FY51	FY52	FY53	FY54	FY55	FY56	FY57	FY58	FY59	FY60
Total	36.6	14.3	11.9	13.2	14.3	45.2	57.2	44.3	30.4	33.8	38.1	39.7	41.1	42.2	40.3

Figure 1: U.S. Department of Defense Total Obligation Authority (TOA) Budgets from FY46-FY60[239]

realistic fiscal approach. The Eisenhower administration deliberately applied this approach

beginning almost immediately to its reworking of the FY1954 budget inherited from the Truman

administration. It did so with a specific intent towards improving the ability of the American

industrial base to meet military demands more predictably, in the right balance, and without the

"premature closing down of production lines with consequent erosion of production potential."[240]

The specific effect of this "plateau" approach in defense spending in the direction of the

industrial base can be seen in Figure 2, which depicts Department of Defense spending in the

combined categories of procurement and research, development, testing and evaluation

(RDT&E). Again, one observes a higher baseline of spending in these categories in the years

following the Korean War armistice. The gradual increase within the post-war plateau seen in

both categories of budgets as depicted in Figures 1 and 2 reflects not only, of course increased

---

[239]Data used in Table 1 derived from U.S. Department of Defense, *National Defense Budget Estimates for FY 2000*, 84-85.

[240]Leighton, *Strategy, Money, and the New Look*, 96.

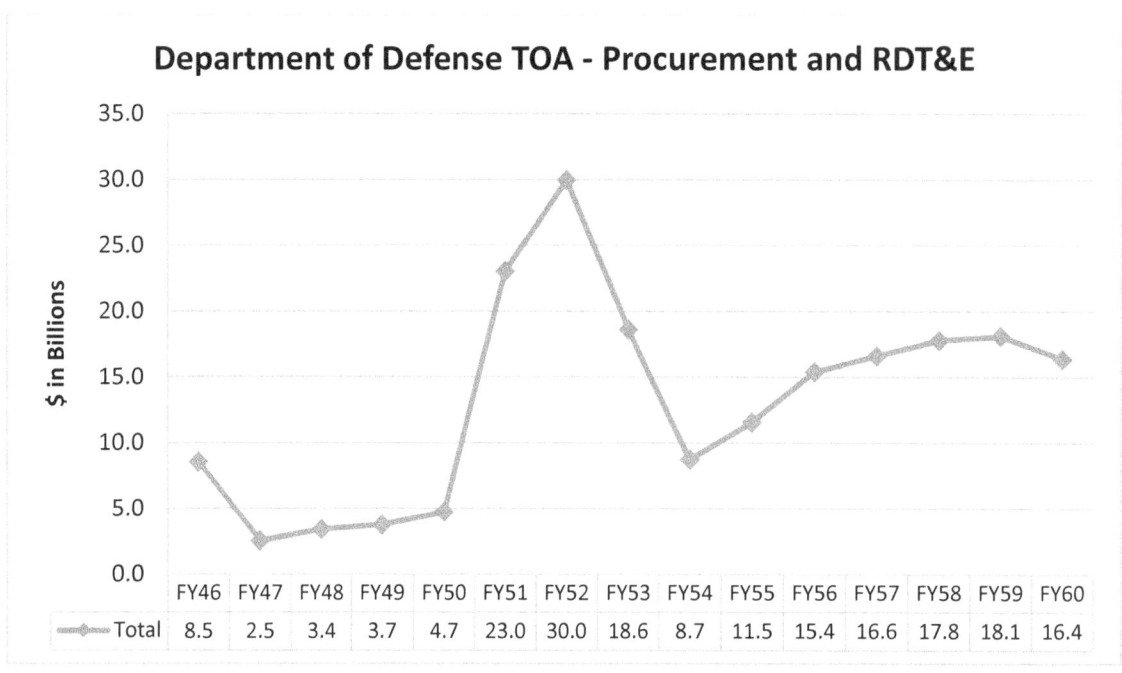

	FY46	FY47	FY48	FY49	FY50	FY51	FY52	FY53	FY54	FY55	FY56	FY57	FY58	FY59	FY60
Total	8.5	2.5	3.4	3.7	4.7	23.0	30.0	18.6	8.7	11.5	15.4	16.6	17.8	18.1	16.4

Figure 2: U.S. Department of Defense Total Obligation Authority Budgets for Procurement, Research, Development, Testing and Evaluation (RDT&E) from FY46-FY60[241]

spending, but an increase in "general price levels," especially after 1955, but also shortened lead times of procured items and improved billing procedures from suppliers.[242]

Thus, the growing dependence of the U.S. military on its national industrial base for the technology and production of superior firepower as demanded by the New Look approach, combined with the unprecedented endstrength of its standing peacetime military, could not permit an overall lower base of spending relative to the most recent interwar period. The level of military and industry intermeshing and interdependence as depicted in the previous section would continue to grow throughout the thirty years of Cold War that followed Eisenhower's presidency and into the Global War on Terror. Nevertheless, Eisenhower provided calm and deliberate leadership, accompanied by fiscal balance and a relative restraint in defense spending. Through a

---

[241]Figures derived by the author by summing each service's Total Obligation Authority (TOA) Procurement and Research, Development, Testing and Evaluation (RDT&E) budgets as listed in the U.S. Department of Defense, *National Defense Budget Estimates for FY 2000*, 144-145, 150-151, 156-157.

[242]Watson, *Into the Missile Age*, 90-91.

combination of political skill, and certainly some luck, Eisenhower remains "the only president in the twentieth century to reside over eight years of peace and prosperity."[243]

CONCLUSION

Although this section presents conclusions that compare and contrast the strategic policies of Presidents Truman and Eisenhower and how these policies affected the U.S. military and its relationship to the national industrial base, these conclusions consider the contexts in which decisions on policy occurred. They do not attempt to compare, impart judgment, and deem either Truman or Eisenhower as the "better" President. It is impossible to determine, for example, how Eisenhower would have conducted the post-World War II military drawdown and reconversion efforts in the specific contexts of the domestic economic and international security framework existing in 1945. It is equally impossible to determine how Truman would have reshaped the military during the period of emerging technology and international events unique to the mid to late-1950s. Thus, these conclusions consider the specific domestic and international contexts addressed in this monograph.

First, Harry Truman entered the office of the Presidency *somewhat* unexpectedly (he was, after all, Vice President). By present day standards, it is fair to say that he did not receive the proper grooming by his predecessor or his administration to fill the role confidently, especially on international issues. Second, the passing of Franklin D. Roosevelt placed Truman in a position to lead an administration that was not only unfamiliar to him, but was developed and managed by his towering predecessor for an unprecedented twelve years. Third, Truman came to power not only confronted with the two unique challenges presented above, but also having to direct significant transitions already underway. A massive war in Europe was ending, a shift to the Pacific theater was imminent, and the role of the United States in the global power structure was

---

[243]Smith, *Eisenhower*, 550.

emerging rapidly. Soon, he would confront the challenges of drawing down the largest military force in American history to date while having to thwart the potential economic pitfalls that accompany such an endeavor. Finally, although the rise and nature of Soviet power during the early interwar years seems obvious to us today, it was not immediately apparent at the time. Thus, Truman was the first president to make decisions as the leader of one superpower in a bipolar world.

In light of this context, Truman's rapid dismantling of the existing massive military structure and shift in priorities and federal expenditure towards more domestic economic and social concerns become more understandable. This approach to post-war policy was standard practice in American history up to this point and Truman likely saw no reason to deviate from it. However, the deceptive and nebulous strategies of Joseph Stalin, himself quite experienced in strategic affairs by 1945, made it difficult for the comparatively inexperienced Harry Truman to visualize, describe or direct a national security strategy to which the military readily could adapt. As the Truman administration recognized the Soviet-led communist challenge to the international system in the later interwar years, it initially chose a one-dimensional "soft power" response with an emphasis on international aid and military assistance, as evidenced by the economic basis of the Truman Doctrine and the Marshall Plan. As a result, the combination of reduced defense spending and vague military strategies characterizing the early years of the Truman presidency left a directionless, poorly trained and emaciated Army that plunged headlong into the Korean War. Furthermore, these same budgetary priorities quickly drove the industrial base into a state of near non-existence. Consequently, the Army found itself in the midst of armed conflict on the Korean peninsula equipped with unbalanced, antiquated and poorly maintained and distributed arms and ammunition. The American industrial base would require many months to overcome its dormancy and provide a consistent and adequate supply of quality arms and ammunition. The evolving policy of containment throughout the interwar years recognized too late, in the spring of 1950, the importance of the military dimension of power in international politics.

In contrast, Eisenhower entered the presidential sphere with the identity and nature of the "enemy" firmly established. Eisenhower also enjoyed the more traditional deliberate introduction to power whereby he could choose and confer with an administrative Cabinet in advance of his inauguration. He possessed international recognition by friends and foes alike as a man of significant experience in international and strategic military affairs and the domestic prestige of a national hero.

The limited nature of the military and industrial mobilizations spurred by the Korean War did not require the drastic reductions by Eisenhower at its armistice in 1953 as those of World War II in 1945. By viewing the overall context as one of an ongoing struggle with communist aggression and a domestic posture of a significant, but not exorbitant, military and industrial mobilization, Eisenhower seized the opportunity to approach the reduction of both military and industrial structures in a stable and deliberate manner. These structures would persist at a level of "limited mobilization," leveling off at a "higher plateau" of unprecedented peacetime military budgets and personnel strengths throughout Eisenhower's presidency. Eisenhower had forever closed the door on America's tendency to rapidly skeletonize the military following involvement in armed conflict.

Furthermore, the Truman policy of containment provided the framework for Eisenhower's New Look. Whereas Truman after 1950 sought to match communist aggression wherever it may appear, Eisenhower sought what was, in theory, the less expensive approach of using nuclear deterrence to prevent it from occurring in the first place. However, as nuclear parity between the superpowers developed, the importance of conventional force reemerged. Under Eisenhower's direction, the form of this conventional force changed to adopt technology and maintain costs, especially in the Army. However, his specific views on the purpose of the Army, in particular, within the New Look framework remained unclear. Both Generals Ridgway and Taylor struggled to match Eisenhower strategic visions with what he considered an appropriate military ground force. Although Eisenhower's approach to national security and defense spending was comparatively stable and consistent relative to that of Truman, it proved too complex for a realistic military adaptation to his views by the Army.

Nevertheless, the pursuit of power projection superiority as desired by Eisenhower's New Look strategy developed in the military an addiction to technology. As the complexity and scale of the Army's dependence on technology quickly evolved into requirements greatly exceeded by its internal capabilities, a vast interwoven and intractable relationship between the Army and its industrial base emerged. It is precisely the form and scale of this relationship, and the potential for the industry "tail" to wag the proverbial military "dog," that seemed to have alarmed Eisenhower near the end of his administration. Eisenhower even seems to have taken responsibility for, or perhaps simply expressed frustration at his inability to moderate, its existence when he issued his now famous and dire warning about the influence of the "military-industrial complex" in his farewell address to the American nation.[244] Although the nature of this relationship remained and even intensified after Eisenhower left office, awkward concepts of military structure, such as the Pentomic division, did not.

In the context of national defense, the philosophical tension running throughout both the Truman and Eisenhower administrations consisted of how best to counter threats to the security of the United States and its Western Allies. The key to strategy development rested in the processes used to recognize the identities and natures of the threats themselves. Although both administrations identified communism and a weak domestic economy as the dual threat of their

---

[244]Paul A. C. Koistinen, *State of War: The Political Economy of American Warfare, 1945-2011* (Lawrence, KS: University Press of Kansas, 2012), 17.

times, they did not agree as to the nature of these threats. As a result, differences in strategies, military structures, and the role of the industrial base prevailed.

What is interesting to note is that both Presidents Truman and Eisenhower began their administrations at the tail end of major armed conflicts originating years before their initial terms in office. They both had to balance their views regarding perceived threats to national security with inherited military structures and strategies within a dynamic domestic and international context. Despite this complexity, they had move a nation forward. In the end, neither Truman nor Eisenhower elucidated a strategic view clear enough for the military to convert into a national military strategy with confidence.

Today, a similar challenge presents itself. While reducing the American presence in Afghanistan, our national leaders strive to balance their perceptions of strategic threats with current force structures in a domestic economic context that requires significant reductions in defense spending but yet an international context that demands our continued leadership. Despite the recent restructuring of our Army into a brigade-centric force during the wars in Iraq and Afghanistan, another restructuring now appears imminent. If the level of military force required for maintaining security persists as defense expenditures decrease, the role of technology may become even more relevant, as it as it did during the Eisenhower years. As the prominence of robotics in most manufacturing production lines demonstrates, technology appears to offer a less expensive, and often times more effective, substitute for human beings. Something must offset the reductions in military endstrength if national leaders simultaneously insist that current military capabilities remain, or even increase. It is likely to be technology that does the offsetting. As a result, ties between select industrial entities and military agencies will likely strengthen.

Only extensive and honest discourse between civilian and military leaders can provide optimal solutions to questions of military endstrength, structure and strategy. As the era of the Truman and Eisenhower presidencies demonstrates, without the context of a clear and attainable national security strategy, realistic answers to questions regarding national military strategy are not possible.

BIBLIOGRAPHY

Akens, David S. *Historical Origins of the George C. Marshall Space Flight Center.* Huntsville, AL: Historical Office, Office of Management Services, George C. Marshall Space Flight Center, National Aeronautics and Space Administration, 1960.

Army Forces Far East and Eighth U.S. Army, HQ. "Logistics Study of the Korean Campaigns, 1950-1953, Vol I." (1954).

Bacevich, Andrew J. "The Paradox of Professionalism: Eisenhower, Ridgway, and the Challange to Civilian Control, 1953-1955." *The Journal of Military History* 61, no. 2 (April 1997): 303-333.

Bergaust, Erik. *Rocket City, U.S.A.: From Huntsville, Alabama to the Moon.* New York: Macmillan, 1963.

Bowie, Robert R., and Richard H. Immerman. *Waging Peace : How Eisenhower Shaped an Enduring Cold War Strategy.* New York: Oxford University Press, 1998.

Condit, Doris M. *The Test of War, 1950-1953.* Washington, DC: Historical Office, Office of the Secretary of Defense, 1988.

Conner Jr., Arthur W. "The Armor Debacle in Korea, 1950: Implications for Today." *Parameters*, (Summer 1992): 11.

Converse III, Elliott V. *Rearming for the Cold War, 1945-1960.* Washington, DC: Historical Office, Office of the Secretary of Defense, 2011.

Cray, Ed. *General of the Army: George C. Marshall, Soldier and Statesman.* New York, N.Y.: Cooper Square Press, 2000.

Davis II, Robert T. *The Challenge of Adaptation: The US Army in the Aftermath of Conflict, 1953 - 2000.* Fort Leavenworth, KS: Combat Studies Institute Press, 2008.

Donovan, Robert J. *Conflict and Crisis: The Presidency of Harry S. Truman, 1945-1948.* Columbia, MO: University of Missouri Press, 1996.

Eisenhower, Dwight D. *The White House Years (Volume 1): Mandate for Change, 1953-1956.* Garden City, NY: Doubleday, 1963.

Epley, William W. *America's First Cold War Army, 1945-1950.* Arlington, VA: Institute of Land Warfare, Association of the United States Army, 1999.

Gaddis, John Lewis. *The Cold War: A New History.* New York: Penguin Press, 2005.

Hamby, Alonzo L. *Man of the People: A Life of Harry S. Truman.* New York: Oxford University Press, 1995.

Harding, Craig A. "Budgeting for the Nation's Defense Following the End of National Conflicts." Master's Thesis, School of Advanced Air and Space Studies, 2009.

Heller, Charles E., and William A. Stofft. *America's First Battles, 1776-1965*. Lawrence, KS: University Press of Kansas, 1986.

House, Jonathan M. *A Military History of the Cold War, 1944-1962*. Norman, OK: University of Oklahoma Press, 2012.

Howard, Bart. "Army Transformation, 1953-1961: Lessons of the "New Look" Army." U.S. Army War College - Army Heritage Collection Online, 2004.

Huston, James A. *Outposts and Allies: U.S. Army Logistics in the Cold War, 1945-1953*. Selinsgrove: Susquehanna University Press, 1988.

Huston, James A. *Guns and Butter, Powder and Rice: U.S. Army Logistics in the Korean War*. Selinsgrove: Susquehanna University Press, 1989.

Kendall, John Michael. "An Inflexible Response: United States Army Manpower Mobilization Policies 1945-1957." Ph.D. Dissertation, Duke, 1982.

Kinnard, Douglas. *President Eisenhower and Strategy Management : A Study in Defense Politics*. Washington: Pergamon-Brassey's, 1989.

Koistinen, Paul A. C. *State of War: The Political Economy of American Warfare, 1945-2011*. Lawrence, KS: University Press of Kansas, 2012.

Lasby, Clarence G. *Project Paperclip: German Scientists and the Cold War*. New York: Atheneum, 1971.

Leffler, Melvyn P. *A Preponderance of Power: National Security, the Truman Administration, and the Cold War*. Stanford, CA: Stanford University Press, 1992.

Leighton, Richard M. *Strategy, Money, and the New Look, 1953-1956*. Washington, DC: Historical Office, Office of the Secretary of Defense, 2001.

McCullough, David G. *Truman*. New York: Simon & Schuster, 1992.

Medaris, John B. *Countdown for Decision*. New York: Putnam, 1960.

Millett, Allan Reed. *The War for Korea, 1945-1950: A House Burning*. Lawrence, KS: University Press of Kansas, 2005.

Osgood, Kenneth Alan. *Total Cold War: Eisenhower's Secret Propaganda Battle at Home and Abroad*. Lawrence, KS: University of Kansas, 2006.

Rearden, Steven L. *The Formative Years, 1947-1950*. Washington, DC: Historical Office, Office of the Secretary of Defense, 1984.

Ridgway, Matthew B., and Harold H. Martin. *Soldier: The Memoirs of Matthew B. Ridgway*. New York: Harper, 1956.

Schnabel, James F. *Policy and Direction: The First Year*. Washington, DC: Office of the Chief of Military History, United States Army, 1972.

Smith, Jean Edward. *Eisenhower: In War and Peace*. New York: Random House, 2012.

Stewart, William G. *From War to Peace: A History of Past Conversions. Annex B to Adjusting to the Drawdown, Report of the Defense Conversion Commission*. Bethesda, MD: Logistics Management Institute, 1993.

Taylor, Maxwell D. *The Uncertain Trumpet*. New York: Harper, 1960.

United States Department of Defense. *National Defense Budget Estimates for FY 2000*. Washington, DC: Department of Defense, 1999.

United States National Archives. *The Public Papers of the President, Dwight D. Eisenhower, 1953*. Washington DC: U.S. Government Printing Office, 1960.

Watson, Robert J. *Into the Missile Age, 1956-1960*. Washington, DC: Historical Office, Office of the Secretary of Defense, 1997.